The Best of the Past®

Preserving and Flying
Aviation's Fifty-Year Legacy

by
Brian M. Silcox

MACH 1, Inc.
Chico, California

MACH 1, Inc.
PO Box 7360, Chico, CA 95927

Images provided by American Design And Marketing, Inc.
Writing Consultant: Jeffrey Baggett
Editorial Assistant: Lindy Hoppough
Set in 15/18 Adobe Garamond

Library of Congress Catalog Card Number: 93–078249

ISBN: 0–929823–14–1

First printing, December 1993

Printed in Singapore by Craft Print Pte, Ltd.

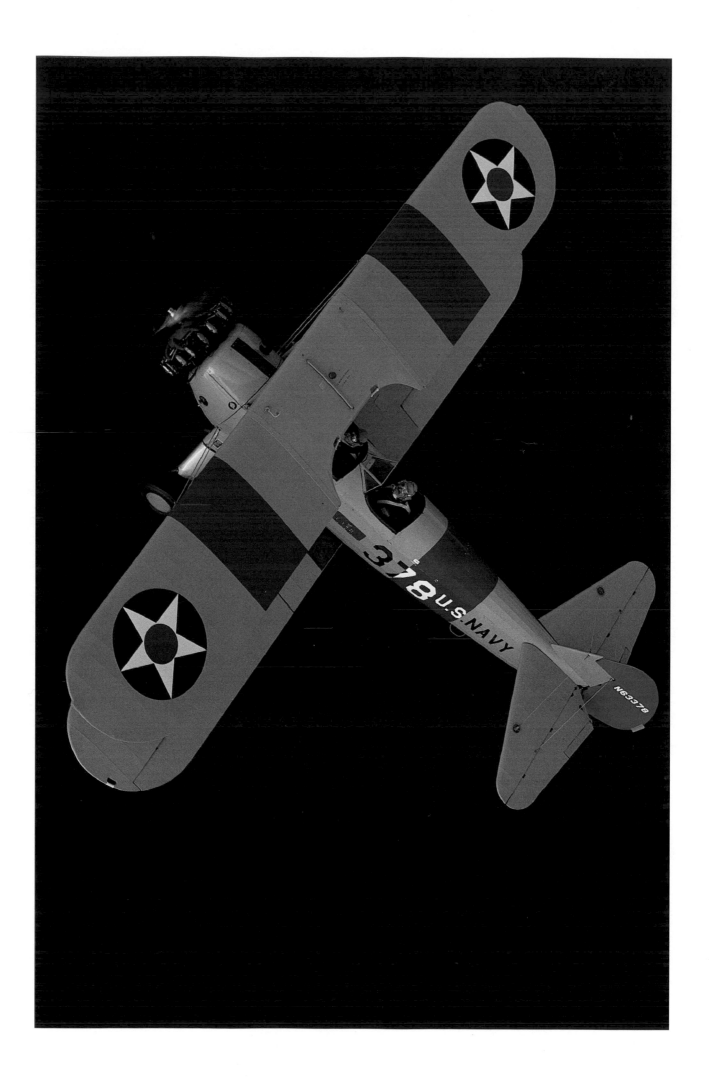

Forward

For four years, Mach 1 has featured Brian Silcox's photographs exclusively in our annual "Best of the Past" calendar. Our customers clamored for "more," and we are pleased to oblige with this book — a fascinating chronicle of Brian's quest to capture these famous vintage aircraft on film. His combined talents as a photographer *and* pilot have given him the unique opportunity to explore his subject fully, not only on film but in flight, at the controls of the classic trainers, fighters and bombers.

As a self-described perfectionist, he is not satisfied with simply photographing airplanes, but capturing their individual personalities — the infectious nostalgic appeal of the powerful warbirds — in the environment where they live and breath: the free domain of the sky.

With a reverence only possible in an individual who has personally experienced the thrill of stalls and spins in the propeller-driven warbirds, and with the excitement of a little boy whose life was changed when he first pondered the photograph of a shiny red Warhawk, Brian has made it his mission to preserve on film the images of the classic warplanes of fifty years past. In his quest — from Marana, Arizona, to Kissimmee, Florida, to Washington, D.C. — Brian has met and flown with a fascinating group of individuals who are dedicated to preserving and flying these remarkable airplanes. They have contributed mightily to his efforts, and this is their story as well as his.

— Paul P. Farsai —
Publisher

Acknowledgments

Whether at the individual level, or in the association of the large organization, thousands of dedicated men and women have contributed to preserve and maintain the spirit of aviation's fifty year legacy. I had the privilege of working with many of these very contributors. It is my sincerest hope that this volume serves to recognize the considerable investment of time, talent and financial resources, which have helped perpetuate this legend in aviation. I would also like to express my personal gratitude to all those who were involved in the creation of these images of *The Best of the Past.*

— Brian M. Silcox —

Contents

The Best of the Past®

Introduction

In the scheme of aviation's first one hundred years the airplane has evolved from the flimsy bi-winged wood and fabric *aeroplane*, to the ultra-modern, computer stabilized transonic jet *aircraft* of the approaching twenty-first century. Probably the most notable development in this process occurred with the advent of all-metal construction technology. During the early 1930s, trends in aerodynamics and engineering fostered a new breed of aircraft, which not only greatly exceeded the performance of the preceding generation of flying machines, but also forecast what shape aircraft of the future would take.

Known as the "Golden Age of Aviation," this transitional period, in a brief ten years' time, brought forth some phenomenal changes. Flight speeds increased from less than two hundred miles per hour, to well over four hundred miles per hour. Tests developed our understanding of the atmosphere and led to aircraft and powerplants capable of operating to altitudes of over forty thousand feet. The shriek of the turbojet engine, first heard in 1937, announced the beginning of a revolutionary new era in aviation. The catalyst for much of this rapid-fire aeronautical advancement was the rumor of war. As Europe felt the rumblings of a resurgent and increasingly militant Germany and Japan's armies rolled through China, military aviation was the impetus for many of the changes to aircraft design and performance.

At the outbreak of war, the frenzied pace of aircraft development saw designs conceived in one month proven obsolete in the next. Out of this process, however, emerged some of the most colorful and prolific creations in the history of flight. Names like *Lightning* and *Marauder* personified the swift and powerful nature of these airplanes, which evolved as the pinnacle of development in propeller-driven aircraft. A labor force of unforeseen potential was mobilized in aircraft factories to produce hundreds of thousands of fighters and bombers to meet the demands of the ever expanding air war. Mighty armadas of long-ranging Liberators, Mustangs, and Flying Fortresses met in battle with hordes of German Focke-Wulfs and Messerschmitts high over the European continent. Meanwhile, halfway around the globe, U.S. Navy Hellcats slugged it out with the Japanese Zero fighters on the fronts of the Southwestern Pacific theater. The fury of the world conflict saw the simultaneous creation and destruction of greater numbers of aircraft than has occurred during any period in the history of flight.

The war's climactic conclusion drew an end to this amazing transitional period. The jet age was dawning, and the huge fleets of warplanes fell quickly into demise. Once feared names such as *Havoc, Avenger,* and *Dauntless,* met their fate in the smelter's furnace, where they were systematically reduced to ingots of scrap metal. Although a fortunate few escaped this destiny, by the late 1950s some of the most famous aircraft of the Second World War were on the verge of extinction. Of the survivors, some were purchased by civilian owners at bargain prices, as government surplus. Aircraft of utility were pressed into service as executive transports, fire fighters, and crop dusters. Fighter planes could be purchased for as little as $1500! The glamourous P-51 Mustang was in demand because of its classic lines and fantastic performance. If you could afford the fighter's ravenous thirst for high octane aviation gasoline, you were in for the ride of your life! The Mustang was in the minority, however; most World War II fighters were simply scrapped.

The fortune of the nearly extinct warbirds has taken a dramatic turn in the past two decades, as many dedicated individuals and organizations have invested heavily to ensure the future of the endangered species. The popularity of the classic fighters, bombers and trainers has caused a general resurgence in their populations, as collectors, entrepreneurs, and enthusiasts alike have scoured the globe in search of every last piece and part of these aircraft. The value of each airplane, indeed each part of each airplane, has skyrocketed according to the laws of supply and demand. A small industry has developed to support the recovery, reconstruction and operational maintenance of a growing fleet of fifty-year-old military aircraft worldwide.

Due to the proliferation of flyable World War II airplanes, many people are now able to experience the unique sounds of the Rolls-Royce Merlin V-12 and Pratt & Whitney R-2800 Double Wasp radial engines. The majestic sight of the Boeing B-17 Flying Fortress and the thrilling speed of the 2000 hp Grumman F8F Bearcat have not been lost to time. As these icons of another era have returned to the skies, it has become important to record their image for future generations. Without question, the time will come when these airplanes will be too valuable to be risked in flight, or too costly to maintain.

Discovery of airplanes came to me at the age of eight or nine, I think. Most everyone takes an interest in some part of the world around them at that impressionable age; I just happened to take an interest in airplanes. The space age was firmly upon us, as could be witnessed by the frequent sonic booms which rocked our homes and schoolrooms. From nearby Edwards Air Force Base, the North American X-15 rocket plane plied the upper limits of the stratosphere and beyond, exploring high speeds and high altitude flight. Many of my friends were similarly occupied with dreams of flight and were fast becoming experts in all of the latest aerospace developments.

My interest in flight took a slightly different direction, however, when I came upon some photographs of the old propeller-driven airplanes of the 1930s and '40s. As my curiosity was piqued, I tirelessly acquainted myself with every make and model of aircraft of the period, pouring over all manner of encyclopedias and directories on the subject. My research soon brought to life the fact that some of these classic airplanes still existed! With great enthusiasm, I read an article in a popular aviation magazine written by a man who had purchased and rebuilt a derelict Curtiss P-40 Warhawk fighter, which was featured in scarlet red on the cover, in an in-flight photograph. The photo made a definite impression on me. The idea intrigued me, that a person could actually own and fly one of these machines! I remember reading another article which described the efforts of a small group of Texans who had dedicated themselves to collecting and flying World War II military airplanes and had declared themselves to be "The Confederate Air Force."

In the nearly thirty years since I first became enamored with the classic warplanes, I have tried to capture the essence of each of these machines' unique personalities on film. Each is an individual sculpture in aluminum and steel, an art form representing another era in time. But, as the propellers begin to turn, and the exhausts belch smoke, these magnificent sculptures take on a more lifelike, even animated, quality. In flight, they are truly in their element. My first experiences with formation flying and photography were no less than breathtaking. It was here, I felt, that these machines should be portrayed and remembered.

This volume presents some images of the more well-known aircraft of the period. Through the kindness and patience of many proud owners and pilots, I was able to realize my goal, capturing many of these aircraft in their natural in-flight element. These people bring before the camera not only beautiful subjects, but unique experiences in the recovery and restoration of each particular aircraft. From the pilot's perspective, each machine presents unique challenges and rewards. Under the guidance of some talented instructors, I was allowed to experience some of these challenges and share some of the rewards and frustrations of flying the classic warplanes. Certainly, this is not a comprehensive coverage of World War II aircraft but, rather, a collection of some of the best examples of the most famous planes still flying. These we have aptly entitled *The Best of the Past.*

— Brian M. Silcox —

Boeing B-17F production line, Seattle, Washington, 1942.

Boeing B-17G "Thunderbird" of Lone Star Flight Museum, Galveston, Texas, 1992.

CHAPTER 1

Flying the Best of the Past

In the 1930s army recruiters offered unmarried young men professional flying careers — "The best aviation training in the world." Because flying an airplane was generally considered to be extravagant and dangerous, incentives were deemed necessary to attract eligible applicants. It was not until the early 1930s that the U.S. government seriously considered developing air power, and by 1941 it had barely begun to build a viable air force. Experience and knowledge in aeronautics was limited, and to embark on a career as a pilot required bravery and a thirst for adventure.

Like many an airplane enthusiast of today, I had long dreamed of what those courageous cadets must have felt occupying the cockpit to undergo flight training. From the observer's point of view, one can only guess what the pilot might see, feel or hear, as the throttle comes forward and the takeoff begins. What about the force of acceleration, the vibration and resonance of the engine and propeller, or the sensitivity of the controls?

After many years of wonder, my curiosity had finally reached its peak, and I set out to answer some of those questions. Working with some of the pilots with whom I had flown photo missions, I proposed a training program which would allow me to experience these famous airplanes from the pilot's perspective. Logically, I tried to follow the same sequence of training as the World War II aviation cadet. Lacking the pressures of a World War to feed my sense of purpose, my training was perhaps a bit less dramatic than the cadet's, but certainly no less challenging or rewarding.

Those Early Years of Flight Training: A Briefing

For a cadet in the 1930s, the Army's flight training program consisted of three levels: primary, basic and advanced. When the student passed the advanced level, his instructor would recommend his training to continue, into either bomber or fighter transition programs. After a demanding thirty weeks, and a total of 210 flight hours, the pilot — a newly commissioned officer — was ready to join a squadron.

Keep 'em Flying

The U. S. Army offers, without expense to you, the best aviation training in the world. This instruction prepares you for a professional career, either civilian or military. You will earn as you learn. The Flying Cadet receives $75 a month, plus uniforms, equipment, board and lodging. Upon graduation, he is commissioned a Second Lieutenant in the U. S. Army Air Reserve, and placed on active duty with the Regular Army Air Corps with pay ranging from $205.50 to $245.50 per month.

How to qualify? You must be between 20 and 27 years of age, unmarried, sound physically. You must have completed two years of college, or pass a written examination covering equivalent work.

U. S. ARMY RECRUITING SERVICE

Visit or write the nearest U. S. Army Recruiting Station or write to the Commanding General of the Corps Area nearest you:

First Corps Area, Boston, Mass.
Second Corps Area, Governors Island, N. Y.
Third Corps Area, Baltimore, Md.

Fourth Corps Area, Atlanta, Ga.
Fifth Corps Area, Fort Hayes, Columbus, Ohio
Sixth Corps Area, Chicago, Ill.

Seventh Corps Area, Omaha, Nebr.
Eighth Corps Area, Fort Sam Houston, Texas
Ninth Corps Area, Presidio of San Francisco, Calif.

Or apply to your local Junior Chamber of Commerce

To accommodate the increasing number of cadets, the Army contracted civilian flight schools to perform the primary phase of flight training. At these civilian flight schools, the student would learn the basics of aerodynamics and meteorology, in addition to a student's initial flight training. Primary flight maneuvers included taxi and takeoff, climbs and turns, descents, stalls and landings. The trainers used for primary training — which included the Boeing PT-13 and PT-17, the Ryan PT-22 and the Fairchild PT-19 — each featured an open cockpit, with two seats arranged in tandem: one for the instructor, one for the student. Communications were crude in the open cockpit arrangement. A "gosport" system allowed the instructor to bellow into a funnel and tube, which was connected to the student's leather headgear. The student, in turn, could respond only by nodding or shaking his head. If he had a question, he was pretty much out of luck. The cadet, therefore, had to be well prepared before he mounted the cockpit.

The most widely used primary trainers were the Boeing PT-13 and PT-17, popularly known as the Stearman (after its designer, Lloyd Stearman). Virtually thousands of aviators started their careers in this biplane. Because of its versatility and sturdy construction, the Stearman was in great demand after the war as a crop duster. Although the veteran biplane can still be seen swooping below the treetops in rural farmlands, by far the majority have been restored to their original military trainer configuration, as show planes.

Boeing PT-13 Kaydet, known popularly as the Stearman.

BASIC TRAINING

After the cadet successfully completed primary training, he was advanced to basic training and introduced to the Vultee BT-13 Valiant. This larger, more powerful trainer, had an enclosed cockpit. Now, the student could use an interphone system to communicate with the instructor. In the Valiant, the cadet would learn how to fly in formation, digest the intricacies of instrument and night flying, and prove his worthiness in aerobatics and navigation. Later, during World War II, basic training was incorporated into the advanced program.

Vultee BT-13B Valiant Basic Trainers.

ADVANCED TRAINING

When the recruit finished basic training, his instructor would recommend he go in one of two directions: those destined to fly fighters went to single-engine advanced training and flew the North American AT-6 Texan; those selected for bomber or transport assignments completed their advanced program in the Curtiss AT-9 Jeep or the Cessna AT-10 Wichita trainer.

The advanced trainers — the AT-6 (Army) and SNJ (Navy) Texan — originated in 1935, the product of the fledgling North American Aviation, Inc. So versatile was this aircraft, that it remained in service with the U.S. Air Force until 1956, and in foreign service until the early 1970s. The T-6, as it is now called, has survived in good numbers, and can be seen at nearly any air show event, restored to its original colors.

North American AT-6 (Army) and SNJ (Navy) Advanced Trainers.

I'm a Cadet!

Tens of thousands of military pilots successfully completed their training program and went on to fly the fighters and bombers. What of the tales of ground loops, stalls and spins? To find out, I set out to obtain several hours of flight instruction in both the Stearman and the Texan. I planned to see just how well these airplanes lived up to their reputations and try to gain competency in takeoffs and landings, normal and aerobatic flight maneuvers, stalls and spins.

As I personally found out, the trainers wouldn't be easily mastered in just a few weeks. Aeronautical engineering was still relatively in its infancy. Most aircraft built during the period featured two main landing gear and a small tail wheel. By its very nature, this tail wheel arrangement makes the aircraft directionally unstable on the ground. Left to their own devices, the "tail draggers," as they are now called, will roll in just about any direction — except straight. When you couple this awkward handling with a landing speed of about sixty miles per hour, you can imagine the potential for accidents. Ground handling, accordingly, was one of the first skills the student was expected to master in the trainer, before being turned loose in a fighter or bomber with substantially heavier weights and higher speeds.

For the primary phase of my program, I reported to Henley Field, just outside the town of Geiger, in western Alabama. The surrounding rural farmland, with its gently rolling grass-covered hills and numerous small lakes and ponds, seemed an ideal setting for my purpose. My instructor was Alan Henley, cattleman and pilot by trade. Henley manages several hundred head of cattle on the family ranch and maintains a sideline interest as the leader of a formation aerobatic air show team. The airport, located on Henley property, consists of a single east-west grass runway, approximately three thousand feet in length and fifty feet wide. Parked in front of an open-sided sheet metal hangar, the blue and yellow Stearman trainer stood ready to indoctrinate yet another neophyte pilot to the ways of the air.

Before my primary training, Henley had kindly provided me with a copy of the pilot's operating handbook — all of thrity-seven pages in length — for the Army model PT-13D. It provided a general description of the airplane, normal and emergency procedures, and some operating performance data. On any other occasion, it might not have proved that interesting, but I was about to fly the plane!

Because it stands nearly ten feet high, the Stearman is, at first, a little imposing. Its body is of mixed wood and steel tubular construction, with all surfaces covered in fabric. Two very stout main landing gear project from the fuselage, directly behind the engine, giving the biplane its characteristically tall stance. Its engine, a 9-cylinder 220 hp Lycoming radial, sits bluntly on the nose without cowling.

I climbed into the front cockpit — where the student normally flew — and looked around. To my left, I found the throttle and fuel mixture quadrant, fuel shut-off, control lock and elevator trim controls mounted to the tube structure. In front of my feet, a pair of rudder pedals incorporated hydraulic toe brakes for the main wheels and also served to steer the tail wheel. In keeping with the airplane's task, its systems are quite simple: the instrument panel displays a total of six engine and flight instruments, which present a refreshing change from the computerized electronics of the modern cockpit. Since Henley's Stearman was equipped with neither an electrical system or a gosport tube, our flight would be without communications. Consequently, before our flight we discussed all of the appropriate procedures and techniques, and we agreed that Henley would intervene on the controls only as necessary.

Starting the 9-cylinder radial engine required teamwork. I remained in the front of the cockpit and held the brakes, while Henley heaved the propeller. He pulled the prop first through several revolutions to remove oil that had accumulated in the

Virtually thousands of aviators started their careers in the Stearman.

bottom cylinders (common to all radial engines), and to provide some fuel to prime several cylinders. When ready for start I simply held the brakes, cracked the throttle slightly and selected the ignition to the BOTH position. As luck was with us, the Lycoming puffed and spat a few times, belched a little blue smoke, and came to life. The fabric-covered biplane vibrated with what seemed an animated enthusiasm, ready to embark for the skies.

With Henley safely aboard, and both of us strapped into lap and shoulder harnesses, I nudged the throttle a little, making the big biplane move straight ahead. It was impossible to see straight ahead though, with the engine blocking my view, so I had to turn slightly, get a glimpse ahead, then turn back in the desired direction. This kind of zigzag maneuvering is pretty much standard taxi procedure for all tail wheel equipped aircraft. To turn, I either pushed on the rudder pedals, which are coupled to the steerable tail wheel or, for sharper turns, applied toe brake on the appropriate rudder pedal. It was a little awkward, but I'd expected the Stearman to be somewhat sluggish on the ground. So far — no surprises and my confidence was intact.

Before takeoff, I performed an engine runup, checked the controls, and signaled to my partner that I was ready. When I pushed the throttle forward for takeoff, the tone of the 220 horsepower engine changed from a gentle hum to a thumping, thunderous roar. The vibration of the engine and airframe seemed to heighten the effect, creating a feeling of tremendous power. Engine torque caused a left turning tendency, which I easily countered with some right rudder. Within a few seconds I felt the air flowing over the flight controls, as the stick developed a bit of resistance. I eased the stick forward, and as the tailplane began to fly, my view over the nose improved greatly. Within seconds, we reached the desired takeoff speed of 60 miles per hour, and a gentle tug back on the stick put us in the air. The controls were light, very responsive, and this was fun!

At full throttle, level flight, the Stearman topped out at 100 miles per hour — not a fast plane. With the power reduced to 2000 rpm for cruise, airspeed indicated about 90 miles per hour. Flying the biplane in this sort of environment, with no radio, no control tower and no traffic was ideal. The absence of these ingredients not only provided a beautiful background, it also allowed me to fly the airplane without the distractions present at most airports.

The airplane had a delightful balance in the controls: the elevator and aileron controls had about the same light response. The open cockpit and the feel of the wind were like a dream of flight. Time for a little fun, I thought. Lowering the nose

Stearman zooming up into a loop.

gently, I descended into an open field and marveled at the blur of grass streaming beneath us. The thrill of flying below the treetops was what barnstorming was all about! Approaching a stand of trees, I gave the stick a quick tug which sent us vaulting over them and into the next field.

Enough fun. It was time to do some regular flight instruction: the slow flight, stalls, steep turns, and such things training flights are made of.

The slow flight was pretty predictable: nose up, mushy, sluggish controls, somewhere around 35 miles per hour, but relatively stable. A fair amount of power was required to maintain level flight in this condition, and an appropriate amount of right rudder, to offset torque and propeller effect. As I eased back on the stick, it shook a little in my hand, approaching the stall, which gave me ample warning that the wings were about to cease flying. When I pulled a little harder on the stick, the stall set in and one wing dropped a little, until I relaxed my grip to let the nose fall below the horizon. The recovery was quick as the wings regained lift and the controls became more responsive. Nothing scary here. Now, for some landings.

The grass runway, some 3000 feet long, was of more than adequate length for the Stearman, even for the beginner. My first approach to the runway seemed fine, until I levelled off above the runway and began the flare to touch down. With almost no forward visibility, I lacked enough depth perception to judge my touchdown. To compensate, I looked over one side of the fuselage, which helped me to judge my height. At about that moment, I noticed the rudder pedals moving actively, but not by my feet. We touched down slightly skewed, nose left, and the airplane jerked to the left before I could correct with rudder. I became keenly aware of the fact that someone else was working the controls. Wow! What did I do wrong? With no means of communication with my instructor, I decided to stop the plane and find out what had happened.

Henley briefly clued me in on how to use my peripheral vision, especially with respect to the moment just before touchdown. Then, off we went for another try. This time, approaching the runway, as the nose came up I concentrated on gazing over both sides of the nose at once. With this technique, I was able to gauge not only drift but height above the ground, and I made a little smoother impact. The crosswind landing presented a challenge even to the experienced aviator, due to the narrow track of the landing gear. I suspect the training "fields" of 1943 were exactly what the term implied, with ample room for the student to zigzag about on takeoff or landing. In today's environment, however, a typical runway may be only about seventy-five feet wide, requiring more precise control.

Naval aviators also began their training in the N2S-5 Stearman.

I had been warned about how easy it is to ground loop one of these airplanes. This embarrassing situation results in the airplane being gyrated about one wing-tip, dragging it on the ground, damaging both the plane and the pilot's pride. The biplane's upper wing has no ailerons, which makes it very susceptible to wind gusts. Henley had cautioned me to hold the stick into the wind on every landing. He warned that if one wing starts to lift after landing, it may be very difficult to stop. Timely rudder control input, or even application of one of the wheel brakes, may be required to keep the Stearman tracking straight on landing. If the student can master these techniques, then he is probably ready to tackle the Advanced Trainer: the AT-6 Texan. Following the flight training pattern of the later war years, I skipped basic training and headed directly into advanced.

ADVANCED TRAINING: THE TEXAN

To the aspiring cadet, learning to fly the North American AT-6 must have been a humbling experience. Larger, more powerful, and certainly more complex than the primary and basic trainers, it offered some of the performance of the fighters which he would soon fly. The Texan was a technologically advanced aircraft with features like retractable landing gear, wing flaps and a controllable pitch propeller. It also had a greenhouse type canopy, allowing the pilot to see in every direction.

For the advanced training phase, I travelled to Conroe, Texas, and met with my new instructor, Glenn MacDonald. MacDonald had been through this training sequence once before, qualifying as a P-47 Thunderbolt pilot in 1945. After the war, he spent some time in the Air National Guard, instructing basic flying in the AT-6, which I felt made him uniquely qualified for my program. I hoped to gain some insight from his experience, in addition to learning as much as possible about the Texan. He graciously agreed to train me with, I noticed, a very suspicious looking smile on his face. I had to wonder what he knew that I didn't.

MacDonald supplied me with his original Air Force issue *Basic Flying Manual* and the *Pilot's Operating Instructions Manual* for the AT-6 airplane. I read through the pertinent sections of each manual the night before our first flight, to have some familiarity with the airplane, its systems and general operating procedures.

Any new plane fills one with a mixture of eager anticipation and not so mild apprehension. With such intensity, I climbed aboard the T-6, my adrenaline flowing. Armed with a head full of partially memorized procedure, and the old standby, common sense, I hoped to pull this flight off with grace. As I sat in the front cockpit,

Navy SNJ-5 Texan explores the ridges and canyons of an early evening cloudscape.

MacDonald stood on the wing and re-explained the engine start to me. I held the starter switch, letting the propeller make several revolutions, then selected the magneto switch to BOTH, and with a sort of sneezing sound, each of the nine cylinders began to fire, almost one at a time. Blue-gray smoke puffed from the exhaust stacks as combustion cleared the residual oil from the bottom cylinders. The propeller spun and carried away the cloud, and the engine settled into an even, rumbling idle. The resonant drone of the radial engine is an essential part of the personality of these airplanes.

Steering the Texan on the ground was, like the primary trainer, a little awkward at first. The tail wheel was steerable in the locked position or fully castering in the unlocked position. Transition from unlocked to locked required a bit of anticipation at first, as I aptly demonstrated by weaving about the ramp, trying to get the hang of it. While taxiing, my forward view was blocked by the nose, requiring, again, a zigzag path down the taxiway. As we neared the runway, MacDonald discussed speed. At excessive taxi speed, he warned, a sudden application of brakes can stand the airplane on its nose.

After a routine engine and control check, I moved onto the runway. Before takeoff, MacDonald gave me one more bit of wisdom: to put my hand on the landing gear lever momentarily, and thus avoid searching for it once we became airborne. I applied takeoff power, 36 inches manifold pressure, and as we rolled forward, the acceleration was not overwhelming — I felt confidently in control of the situation. As the tail flew off, the runway came into view over the nose and, almost simultaneously, we reached the desired speed for liftoff. I fumbled a bit with the landing gear lever, pulling it toward my left knee, then back, to retract the wheels.

After takeoff, I reduced the power for climb, setting both the throttle and propeller controls. As I began to relax and enjoy the moment, MacDonald brought the intercom to life with a string of instructions, mostly relating to things we had discussed just before getting into the airplane. So much for pulling this off with grace, I thought, as MacDonald continued, "Look from side to side . . . you can't see over the nose . . . let go of the stick, use your trim . . . ."

So this is what the cadet must have felt like! But there was no time for regret. I began to develop a feel for the airplane, climbing and turning, leveling off, then turning again. When I began to feel comfortable, MacDonald was ready for me to attempt a series of routine training maneuvers: slow flight handling and stalls.

Stalls were not so docile in the Texan. Warning was ample, with some shuddering and shaking, but the wing quit flying fairly abruptly, usually one wing before the

A pair of AT-6G Texans joining formation over the west Alabama woodlands.

other, resulting in a rather disconcerting tendency to snap roll. Recovery was a little sluggish, as the airplane was heavy and took a second or two to regain airspeed. We investigated the stall in both clean and landing configurations, and I was satisfied that I could anticipate the stall and make an effective recovery. Turning for the airport, I let the nose fall below the horizon and watched with excitement as the airspeed increased to 200 miles per hour.

My first landing resulted in a light skip, but I was able to recover into a three-point touchdown. Applying the brakes gently, I tried to make a turnoff while still moving a little too fast. MacDonald duly counseled me about the possibility of a ground loop under these circumstances — I should have slowed to a brisk walking speed. My taxi to the ramp was a rather jerky attempt. I demonstrated that I needed plenty of practice in maneuvering this airplane on the ground.

Over coffee, we took a short break for debriefing. I was anxious to do some landings, since this was part of the legend of the Texan, but my instructor suggested we first do some more air work, including spins and aerobatics. We briefed the spin entry and recovery techniques, and I felt reasonably well prepared to execute the maneuver. MacDonald recommended that I make the second flight from the back seat, to try to cure any remaining tendency to look over the nose during landings. He felt that the back seat offered more challenge, actually forcing me to use my peripheral vision.

To set up for the spins, we climbed to nine thousand feet, and I slowed the Texan to the onset of the stall. Just prior to the stall, I pulled the stick all the way back, and abruptly pushed the left rudder pedal to its limit. I anticipated an abrupt snap to the left, but found the entry much less dramatic than I had expected. After the first turn, however, I was rewarded: with a ferocity I could not have foreseen, the airplane wrapped itself into a dizzying spin as the rate of rotation nearly doubled! I applied full opposite rudder, as recommended, and as the rotation rate decreased, I gave a good forward thrust on the stick. In my excitement, however, I forgot to let go with the opposite rudder, and the airplane responded by abruptly entering a spin in the opposite direction! "Nice job," I thought to myself, as my instructor regained control of the airplane. I tried the spin one more time — following the procedure more carefully — which yielded a smarter, less panicked recovery. Until you've seen the spin once, you really have no idea of what you're in for. This particular exercise taught a valuable lesson about the T-6 but was also a very humbling experience.

During our return to the airport I tried a couple of barrel rolls. Like many other airplanes, the T-6 requires a dive to gain enough airspeed for the maneuver. The

Diving to begin the roll . . .

. . . the view through the greenhouse canopy is spectacular . . .

. . . as the horizon falls away,
rolls and rises.

barrel roll is a very graceful combination of pitch and roll, which describes a spiraling path through the air. The maneuver is particularly challenging for the student, because as the roll progresses, both airspeed and control forces are constantly changing. The student must refer to the outside references to maintain a constant rate of pitch and roll. Through the Texan's long greenhouse canopy, the view is both spectacular and exhilarating as the horizon falls away, rolls, and rises again. Properly executed, the maneuver should end at the same altitude as it was begun. On my second try, I felt I had come pretty close and smiled, as I thought momentarily of what someone had once described to me as "seat of the pants" flying.

Because these kinds of maneuvers involve great stress on the airplane, the designers at North American seriously anticipated the demands for structural integrity in the T-6. More than once, a student like me has erred in his maneuver, only to recover in a screaming dive, pulling a few too many Gs.

Re-entering the traffic pattern, I tried to plan ahead for the landing approach and began to configure the flaps and landing gear. I had not anticipated the fact that the runway would be all but impossible to see over the nose, from the back seat. By lowering the nose and making a steeper glide, I found I could keep the runway in sight reasonably well, but this caused an increase in speed, which was one more problem for me to work with as I began the flare. On touchdown, I bounced back into the air, the wings still flying with plenty of excess airspeed. As I attempted to settle back onto the runway, I felt the throttle come forward, and a waggle of the stick, as MacDonald, his patience exhausted, took control.

Knowing what had caused the bounce, I resolved to put the error behind me and try again. On the next approach, I set up the steeper glide path farther from the runway and stabilized the airplane earlier in the approach at the desired 80 miles per hour. This time, I was tracking straight and under control as I flared to the three-point attitude. Just before touchdown, I gently brought the stick all the way into my lap, judging my height to be just above the pavement. All three wheels impacted positively, but we remained firmly on the ground. MacDonald had recommended the three-point, or full stall landing technique, as it would provide positive directional control with the steerable tail wheel immediately after landing. During the roll-out, I found that the T-6 needed an aggressive reign on the rudders to keep it tracking straight ahead. In a similar fashion to the Stearman, the narrow track of the main landing gear seems to aggravate this situation.

For my third and last flight in the Texan, the objective was crosswind landings, using the "wheel landing" technique. Wheel landings are made by making the touch-

Lone Star Flight Museum's immaculate Harvard Mk IV in colorful Royal Canadian Air Force markings.

down on the two main wheels, and keeping the tail up, using the rudder for directional control during the roll-out. Of the airport's three runways, we selected the one which was oriented perpendicular to the wind, to get the most benefit from this exercise. I found no difficulty in the wheel landing; however, as the tail was lowered during roll-out, the airplane tended to "weather vane" rather abruptly into the wind. On one such landing, the airplane veered sharply left, nearly leaving the runway when my partner mashed the right brake to avoid the impending ground loop. I had pushed the rudder pedal to the stop, but this had no effect on the swerving plane. As I quickly learned, under these circumstances, the deliberate use of one of the wheel brakes may be the only way to maintain directional control. I also learned to fly the tail to the ground while sufficient airspeed remained to control the rudder and elevator through the transition. This incident was another lesson in humility, clearly demonstrating the need for proper technique and constant vigilance with the T-6. I had been warned that this would eventually happen, and I was grateful not to have experienced the ground loop with it.

There's no doubt about it: the Texan is a demanding airplane to fly. It's tricky on landings, doesn't tolerate poor technique, and it exaggerates any problems in control. This is exactly why the Texan was noted for being an excellent trainer. I had been told by more than one person that if I could master the AT-6, then the P-51 Mustang would be no problem.

FIGHTER TRANSITION: THE MUSTANG

After advanced training, the cadet graduate was about to reach his goal: flying a single-seat pursuit airplane, capable of speeds in excess of 400 miles per hour and reaching lofty altitudes of some 40,000 feet. With his shiny new wings of silver, the newly commissioned second lieutenant was off to complete the final phase of his training.

Transition from the AT-6 to the high performance single-seater offered a serious challenge to the cadet. As the newer models emerged, early model Curtiss P-40 fighters had been relegated to the training role and were typically the student's first single-seat aircraft. The cadet would undergo a curriculum which included a thorough ground school on the airplane and its systems, spending enough hours in the cockpit memorizing the location and operation of switches and controls that he could likely perform his tasks blindfolded. When he had been checked on his knowledge of the airplane and procedures, and his instructor had supervised the engine start, the new fighter pilot was sent on his way.

Many of these pilots found the P-40 to have several undesirable characteristics. The fighter's long nose provided even less forward visibility than the AT-6. Additionally, the P-40's liquid-cooled Allison engine could not endure prolonged taxi time, as its coolant temperature would quickly reach its red-line value. Although it was about the same size as the AT-6, the P-40 weighed nearly twice as much, giving it a miserable climb rate. By far, the greatest challenge the new pilot faced was the handling of some 1400 horsepower. A sudden application of power could easily cause a complete loss of directional control, due to the fantastic torque it created. To help reduce the number of training accidents, in the later stages of the war, the Army developed dual-control versions of the P-40N Warhawk and, later, of the P-51D Mustang. Under appropriate supervision, the transition became a safer proposition.

Today, the recommended procedure for checkout in a World War II fighter airplane is to fly a dual-control version with someone who knows the airplane. Although many dual-control versions of the fighters are flying today, only one is commercially available for this purpose. The Stallion 51 Corporation of Kissimmee, Florida, offers a complete transition course in their TF-51 Mustang, *Crazy Horse*. They also offer a hands-on orientation flight for those who simply want to experience the most famous fighter of World War II. With this in mind, I contacted Stallion 51 to experience the transition from the advanced trainer to the fighter.

The full transition course at Stallion 51 is eight flights, the course averaging about fifteen total hours of flying. After the second flight, if the student performs well, he moves up to the front seat for the completion of the course. The student learns all aspects of flying the P-51, including normal and aerobatic maneuvers, stalls and spins. Aerobatic training makes the student pilot familiar with unusual attitudes and appropriate recovery techniques. Stall and spin training take the student a step further into departure from controlled flight. Both are an integral part of high performance military flying. If desired, one can also request combat maneuvers and formation training.

Stallion 51's instructional talents stem from the professional backgrounds of their two pilots, Doug Schultz and Lee Lauderback. Shultz originally purchased the Mustang in 1987 to use for commercial flight training. In 1988, Lauderback joined him to form the present company. Schultz served with the U.S. Navy, including two combat tours in Vietnam, flying the F4 Phantom. He was instrumental in the conception and development of the Navy's fleet adversary squadron, which was

North American P-51D Mustangs
in formation over Northern Indiana.

devised for realistic air combat training. Lauderback, formerly chief pilot of Arnold Palmer's corporate aviation interests, brings both professional flying and management skills to the operation.

Schultz and Lauderback aren't trying to train pilots for air show or aerobatic demonstration flying but, rather, they want to help pilots gain proficiency in the high performance environment. Greater proficiency, they hope, will promote safer operation of the remaining World War II fighter aircraft.

Stallion 51 is highly rated by many current Mustang owners and pilots who have gone through the program, using it for transition or annual proficiency training. Also, the Navy Test Pilot School at Patuxent River, Maryland, contracts with the Stallion 51 Corporation each year for a portion of their test pilot candidates' aircraft evaluation program.

The full-time commercial operation of the P-51 is no small feat in itself. While the average privately owned World War II fighter is flown about fifty hours annually, Stallion 51's *Crazy Horse* logs between 250 and 300 hours each year. The Packard-built Rolls-Royce Merlin engine averages about five hundred hours between overhauls. The company budgets each overhaul at $100,000, which includes costs for removal, crating, shipping, overhaul and reinstallation. Peter and Richard Lauderback perform all maintenance, supporting three engine cores: one being flown, one in overhaul, and one as a ready spare. Lee Lauderback estimates that for every hour the Mustang is in the air, it requires approximately ten hours of maintenance, including preflight inspections, general maintenance, annual inspections, engine overhaul and cleaning. As in any commercial aviation venture, appropriate maintenance resources play a major role.

BRIEFING

I met Lee Lauderback at Stallion 51's facility, near the Kissimmee airport, to brief for my transition flight. Lauderback led me into a small classroom equipped with video and slide presentations of airplane systems and cockpit procedures training. In an adjacent room, a cutaway Merlin engine was mounted for teaching the associated engine systems. Lauderback wanted to know about my experience with the Stearman and the Texan, and about what I hoped to accomplish in my flight in the P-51. I recognized his instructional talent by the thorough nature of his preflight briefing. Based on our conversation, we agreed on some exercises which would highlight some of the problems pilots might have encountered in the fighter transition.

Captain William T. Whisner's P-51D "Moonbeam McSwine," patrolling the southern Illinois countryside.

In the comfort of the classroom, we discussed many of the characteristics of the P-51, mostly concerning its tremendous horsepower and the various effects of its huge propeller. I could feel the anticipation building as the briefing continued, and I recalled my first air show, nearly thirty years ago, in Bakersfield, California, when I stood admiring the P-51 for the first time. I could remember the crackling sound of its engine, its graceful spiraling barrel rolls, and its ability for vertical acceleration. Images of the P-51 from that first air show had inscribed my mind with aeronautical wonder. Now I was preparing to fly it.

Lauderback played a videotape for me which was recorded by a unique recording system mounted aboard the airplane. The system has a remote sensor, mounted to the top of the vertical fin, which provides a forward-facing perspective, encompassing the entire airplane and the horizon. By using videotapes of a student's performance, Lauderback can do a thorough debriefing, covering every facet of the flight that needs to be addressed.

After briefing, we left the classroom and found the airplane prepared for flight. Lauderback demonstrated the exterior preflight inspection, pointing out several items covered in the briefing. I climbed into the rear cockpit and took a few moments to adjust to the fighter's layout. Over each shoulder, the wings appeared to be short. Looking forward, the nose loomed beyond the front cockpit, offering virtually no forward vision. I put my hands on the stick grip and the throttle lever, with a reverent anticipation of what they could accomplish. Lauderback, noticing perhaps a grin on my face, asked if I was ready to strap on the harnesses and cover some emergency bailout procedures. When we finished, Lauderback climbed into the front seat and secured himself in the cockpit, while I, full of adrenaline, did my best to relax.

TAKEOFF

The starter was engaged and the whole airframe jerked as the propeller blades began swinging with increasing speed. The sleeping Merlin awakened as one stack after another of the engine's twelve exhaust stacks puffed smoke. In seconds, the still silence of the cockpit transformed into a crackling staccato and the vital signs began to register: oil pressure, coolant temperature, fuel pressure. The Mustang's hydraulic veins pressurized and the wing flaps responded to the selected UP position. As we began to move, Lauderback greeted me on the intercom system: "OK . . . you have the airplane."

Dual cockpit arrangement of the TF-51 Mustang, "Crazy Horse."

Stallion 51's TF-51 offers the exhilarating experience of World War II's most famous fighter.

This much power demands a certain amount of respect. I carefully nudged the throttle forward, unsure of its sensitivity. At first, I handled everything gingerly: the rudder pedals, the brakes, the throttle. My apprehension faded as I got a better feeling for the controls for taxi. I gained more confidence and gave a bolder push on the throttle to pick up taxi speed. Following Lauderback's taxi instructions, we arrived at the intended runway, and my concentration level had just about peaked. After checking the magnetos and cycling the propeller, Lauderback reviewed the before-takeoff checklist and asked me to taxi onto the runway.

Torque was my greatest concern for takeoff. Lauderback's instructions now came in a steady stream: "As briefed, hold the brakes and advance to 2300 rpm . . . gently release the brakes and come up to 35 inches manifold pressure . . . use your peripheral vision to keep it straight." My attention darted back and forth from runway to manifold pressure gauge, as I juggled the power and steering requirements. The intercom crackled, "OK . . . there's 50 knots, now ease forward on the stick . . . nose a little lower, now come up on the power . . . more power . . . more power, there's 50 inches, you can rotate any time." At 50 knots, the tail came off and my attention was squarely focused outside on the runway center line. I achieved the desired takeoff power when we were at 100 knots. At that point, I responded to the call to rotate and eased back on the stick to make the airplane fly.

And fly it did! I lifted off at 110 knots, and as the wheels tucked into the wings, the airplane lunged forward. The sensation of acceleration was heightened by the blur of concrete streaking by beneath us. The Mustang, subject of years of wonder, was now firmly in my grasp and charging through a thousand feet in stride. As the ground fell away, the perceptions of speed and acceleration faded into the ordinary. The view of the sky and horizon were no less than spectacular, though, as the bubble canopy provided a panavision of the cumulus clouds and Florida landscape.

The intercom crackled in my ears, bringing me back to the matter at hand: a power reduction, trim requirements, airspeed for climb and an after-takeoff checklist. The mechanical and procedural aspects of flying are an unavoidable ingredient of flight training. This was not just a joy ride. I carefully moved the big throttle handle aft (it seemed fit for a locomotive), to set 46 inches of manifold pressure, then eased the propeller control back to 2700 rpm. As we climbed, I plied the sensitivity of the stick, with increasingly steep turns to the right and left, and soon discovered the need for rudder coordination. I rolled left to thirty degrees bank, then right to forty-five degrees . . . then left again to sixty degrees. The steeper banks required

The Mustang's sleek form
is evident in this frontal view.

some muscle on the stick. I pulled the stick farther back to tighten the turn and was surprised by the gentle bumping of the stall buffet.

Rolling wings level, Lauderback asked me to bring the nose up to thirty degrees and hold it. I fixed the nose on a patch of clouds as we explored the effects of the big propeller at diminishing airspeeds. As the airspeed bled off, the nose started to drift left. Soon I had pushed the right rudder pedal against the stop, with the nose still drifting to the left. Abruptly lowering the nose caused it to swing back to the right again. I pictured myself chasing a Focke-Wulf 190 in a climb and having to think and decide, "Uh . . . right rudder?" In combat, one doesn't have such luxury — maneuvering has to be instinctive.

Lauderback, carefully pacing me, invited me to loosen up a bit and maneuver the airplane as I wished. I made a series of lazy eights, with increasing pitch and bank, but my partner coaxed me for more vertical penetration, to show what the fighter could do. I pitched to forty-five degrees, nose up, and just let it climb. And, yes, it did climb! I held the stick all the way to the right and smiled as the horizon smoothly rotated in the bubble. Wow!

STALLS

The warm-up had been fun, but everything has its price, and we needed to spend time in the training routine of slow speed handling and stalls. Lauderback had an extensive repertoire of stalls, in many configurations and attitudes, and we would perform at least eight or nine of them.

When performed with good rudder coordination, the Mustang gives noticeable warning at the onset of the stall. On the other hand, with poor rudder coordination, the pilot can quickly find himself inverted! To begin, Lauderback demonstrated, executing a stall in a left turn with excessive left rudder. Without much buffeting, the airplane abruptly snap-rolled to the left as the stall occurred. "Not the thing to do in the traffic pattern," I thought.

One of the more unusual stall exercises involved pitching the nose up to forty-five degrees, then rolling inverted and pulling into the stall buffet. In this case, we simply reached the onset of the stall and continued the split-S maneuver with repeated pulls into and out of the buffet. As the airplane accelerated down the back side of the maneuver, less stick force was required to achieve the stall buffet. These were the kinds of maneuvers that prepared the transitioning fighter pilot for stalls in a

The visual presentation of the Mustang's bubble canopy is spectacular in aerobatic maneuvers.

changing and unusual attitude and airspeed combination, maneuvers he would need to master before entering into combat.

In my reading of the combat experiences of P-51 pilots, I have found that maximum maneuvering performance was frequently on the edge of the high speed stall, where predictable stall characteristics were the advantage needed for success. Today, to safely operate a fighter like the Mustang, a pilot needs to recognize the stall characteristics in any configuration or speed — and recognize appropriate recovery techniques. Stallion 51's curriculum is specifically aimed at eliminating accidents by concentrating on thorough familiarity with all of the Mustang's stall characteristics.

FIGHTER AEROBATICS

To begin the aerobatic sequence, Lauderback advised, "Enter the loop at 270 knots and use a four-G pull . . . ." To achieve entry speed, I lowered the nose and began the pull at eight thousand feet. My partner kept me informed of my progress, "OK . . . three-and-a-half . . . there's four Gs . . . passing through the vertical, 200 knots . . . over the top, now twelve thousand feet and 100 knots." From the top of the bubble canopy, the horizon came into view and I relaxed the pull slightly. The plunge down the backside of the loop mirrored the climb, emerging at the bottom with a little excess speed at 300 knots on the airspeed indicator. We had traversed four thousand feet of altitude through the loop.

We continued the sequence with some barrel rolls, an Immelmann, Cuban eights and a vertical roll. Each maneuver presented new challenges in control coordination and situational awareness. The power and climb performance, and the spectacular visual presentation of the bubble canopy, contribute to the Mustang's reputation as a pilot's airplane. With entry speeds of 270 knots, however, we had only begun to explore the capability of the plane's vertical performance. In combat, the airplane routinely maintained maneuvering speeds in excess of 400 miles per hour!

The stress of high G maneuvering had taken its toll on my body. This was something I really hadn't anticipated. No preconception I might have had about flying the Mustang included the dry mouth, queasy stomach, and light-headedness I felt as we started back toward the airport for landing. Nevertheless, the lesson made it clear to me that this was part of the reality of flying a high performance military airplane. The fighter pilots of World War II engaged in combat without the luxury of the modern G-suit, and they consequently suffered the effects of their high spirited maneuvering.

Low over the Mississippi River, the Mustang pilot
tracks the horizon through the top of the bubble.

LANDINGS

The approach for landing begins miles from the airport. By design, the Mustang gives up speed grudgingly, so reducing speed requires extra time and distance. We levelled at one thousand feet above the airport and passed overhead at 180 knots. Strategy and judgement play an important part in configuring the airplane for landing. We entered the pattern with a steep left turn to parallel the runway. The steep turn helped to bleed off airspeed to 150 knots, the maximum speed for operating the landing gear. Once the landing gear were extended, they served as a sort of speed brake. The plan was to pass the end of the runway at one thousand feet, 140 knots, with the landing gear down. From this point, we started a descent and a left turn toward the runway. In increments, the flaps were added to further reduce airspeed.

My first approach ended up a little high and fast, so I reduced power. Settling back down onto a normal glide path, I nudged the power back up and checked my speed at about 120 knots — still a bit fast. For the first approach, our target was 110 knots, over the beginning of the runway. I eased the power back some more and let the airplane glide to within a few feet of the ground before closing the throttle. Gently, I eased the stick back, beginning the flare, and awaited the impact of the main wheels. When the wheels finally met the runway surface, I eased the stick forward, holding the tail up, and worked the rudder pedals to track the runway center line. The wide track of the landing gear helped make this job much easier than in the AT-6. Lauderback reset the trim and retracted the flaps, as I pushed forward on the throttle to take off again.

The properly executed landing approach is a matter of judgement and timing, one of the goals being to minimize power changes, which tends to complicate things. My second approach to the runway was closer to the target, arriving over the end of the runway on speed and glide path. Without excessive speed, the airplane settled to the runway more rapidly and touchdown followed almost immediately. As I rolled straight ahead, working the rudder pedals, the intercom crackled with familiar instructions: "Fly the tail down to the runway . . . use your peripheral vision, don't look to one side . . . keep the tail coming down." I released the forward pressure on the stick to let the tail wheel contact the runway and simultaneously switched to use my peripheral vision, correcting for a slight drift to the right. Lauderback called for a gentle application of the brakes, which effectively slowed the airplane.

After slowing to 150 knots, the landing gear can be extended for landing.

The Mustang proved to be easier to fly in many respects than the advanced trainer. Perhaps the reason for my relative success in the Mustang was because the Texan had prepared me well for techniques I used while operating the fighter. That is not to say that the P-51 didn't have its own set of challenges. The Mustang was every bit the performer I had expected. Things happen fast and require timely reactions. I could only imagine how excited and nervous a young cadet must have felt if he'd had to make this transition without the benefit of an instructor.

Taxiing back to the ramp in the usual zigzag pattern, Lauderback asked, "So, what do you think of the Mustang?" I hesitated for several moments, finding I didn't have a simple answer. Certainly, descriptions of speed, power, acceleration and visibility entered my mind. But what really had my tongue tied was the fact that my body had been physically conquered by the experience. A fighter pilot in 1943 was trained with many hours of practice in combat maneuvering: daily exercises, during which he could become accustomed to the stresses of high speed and high-G forces. The pilot was also much younger — probably nineteen years old and in peak physical condition. In one hour and twelve minutes, I gained a much greater appreciation for the expertise, stamina and training of the World War II fighter pilot.

Turning final approach, the pilot targets
for an airspeed of 110 knots.

I had now tried my hand at the trainers and the transitional pursuit plane that prepared fighter pilots for combat. There was, however, one more challenge: the Boeing B-17, a four-engine heavy bomber. At the time of World War II, the Boeing B-17 represented an entirely new classification of large aircraft, and certainly no trainer existed which could functionally prepare the cadet for what he was about to encounter as he made the transition. I was given the opportunity to fly the famous Boeing Flying Fortress and gain some ideas about what the pilot might have felt when he took the controls for the first time.

Few aircraft manufacturers have simultaneously set the pace of technology, broken new ground in design and construction, *and* achieved commercial success. In 1930, the Boeing Company, in Seattle, Washington, flight tested a new monoplane design of all metal construction, featuring a retractable undercarriage. Boldly utilizing unproven design and construction techniques, the company helped to establish the standards of aircraft design which would revolutionize the industry worldwide, but, at that time, without significant sales.

In 1934, against a political tide of isolationism, the leaders of the U.S. Army pursued a doctrine of strategic high altitude bombing, in response to the developing turmoil on the European continent. Issuing a proposal to manufacturers for the design and construction of a new bomber, the Army stated requirements far in excess of the capabilities of existing aircraft. To meet these requirements, Boeing submitted a design utilizing four powerplants, instead of the usual two. Not necessarily a larger

Between the B-17's four throttles, a placard gives power setting
and fuel consumption — between 200 and 300 gallons per hour.

The cockpit of Evergreen Venture's Boeing B-17G "Flying Fortress."

plane, the model 299 was simply twice as powerful as its contemporaries. Boeing was taking a considerable gamble, since the airplane's cost was roughly twice that of its competitor's.

The bomber's public debut, in July 1935, with its multiple machine gun stations, prompted one Seattle newspaperman to call it a "Flying Fortress." While far ahead of its competitors in technology and capability, it would be several years before the fledgling "heavy" would mature into the famous four-engined *Flying Fortress*, ranging the skies over Europe. Modifications and upgrades increased the size of the engines, stretched the fuselage, and improved the defensive armament. The Wright Cyclone 9-cylinder radial engines incorporated the new turbocharger technology, allowing them to operate at altitudes in excess of thirty thousand feet. Much new ground was to be broken before all of the plane's systems could function properly in the harsh cold environment of the substratosphere.

Boeing's initial combat experience over Europe demonstrated that the bombers needed greater defensive armament. One such improvement was the automated Sperry ball turret mounted to the plane's underside. The ball turret provided a single defensive position which could defend the entire underside of the aircraft. Once the bomber was airborne, the gunner took his place in the turret, and was locked within it until one of his fellow crew members released him. Being fully enclosed within the ball, the gunner moved with the guns which were powered by electric motors. Using a pair of levers overhead, the gunner could swiftly rotate and elevate the twin 50-caliber machine guns to any direction he required.

The later model B-17s normally had ten persons aboard, including two pilots, a bombardier, a navigator, one radio operator, a flight engineer, and four gunners — two in the waist, one in the tail and one in the ball. To improve its defense against head-on attacks, the last version of the bomber, the B-17G, harbored under its nose a pair of 50-caliber guns in a hydraulically powered turret. This version of the Fortress featured a total of thirteen machine guns. The fully loaded bomber weighed some 65,000 pounds for takeoff, carried a maximum of 8,000 pounds of bombs, and cruised at 180 miles per hour for a range of 2,000 miles at an altitude of 35,000 feet.

After a B-17 pilot had graduated from advanced multi-engine school, he entered a transition program which included over one hundred hours of four-engine flying, and then he enrolled in ten more weeks of post-graduate ground school. Only then was the three-hundred-hour aircraft commander considered ready for the rigors of combat over Germany.

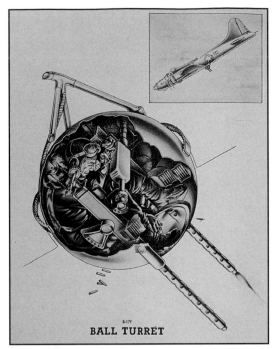

BALL TURRET

A page from the U.S. Army's
maintenance familiarization manual
depicts the ball turret gunner's position.

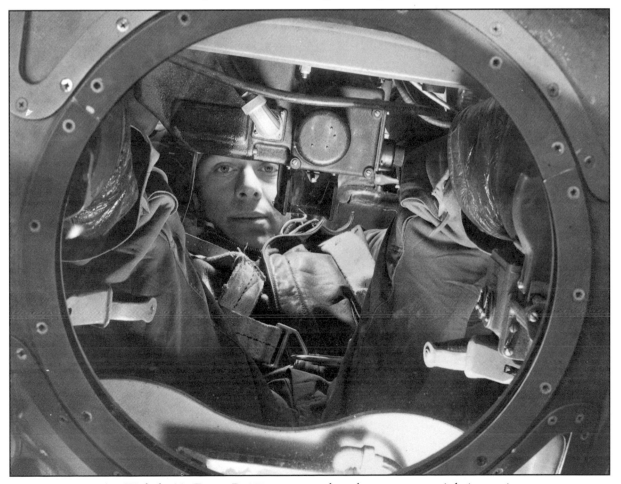

An Eighth Air Force B-17 crew member demonstrates sighting twin
50-caliber guns in the cramped ball turret.

To appreciate the challenges the heavy bomber presented to the twenty-year-old pilots, I accepted an invitation from Bill Muszala of Evergreen Ventures to join him on a maintenance test flight in the Boeing, at their facility in Marana, Arizona.

TAKEOFF

Climbing aboard the Boeing was a gymnastic exercise. I began by gripping the edge of the opening overhead and then hoisted my legs and torso up through the hatch and into the belly of the airplane. I moved aft through a passageway, below and between two pilot seats, from where I could finally climb up into the control cabin. As I got oriented to the inside of the plane, Greg Klein, who served as our engineer/observer, briefed me on the layout of the systems, controls and indicators in the cockpit.

Just as I got settled in my seat, I was startled by a loud squealing noise. Klein had turned on the three battery master switches which activated the hydraulic system. A single electric pump behind the copilot's seat provided 800 psi hydraulic pressure to operate the wheel brakes and engine cowl flaps. The flight controls, conversely, were operated manually, by a series of direct linkage cables and pulleys. The pilots operated the landing gear and wing flaps by electric motors, with normal electrical power provided by four engine-driven generators in flight.

As we performed our preflight inspection, Klein showed me a handcrank which was used to manually extend or retract the landing gear, adding that it required only 248 turns to extend each main wheel. Now I knew the real reason they had brought me along!

In the control cabin, with a kind of reverence, I occupied the pilot's position. It wasn't very comfortable — military cockpits never are — but it was at least roomy enough to avoid bumping any sharp edges with the head or elbows. My view of the ground outside was limited, the nose being long, with a rather prominent Plexiglas dome directly in the pilot's field of vision. Out to the left, I could see forward pretty well and had a great view of engines number one and two.

It was time to start the engines. Klein reviewed the start procedure, similar to all large radial engines, prior to the onset of noise. Unlike the original B-17 pilots, we donned modern headsets to enjoy the convenience of the voice activated intercom, and then performed the before-start checklist: "Batteries, inverters, cowl flaps, generators, hydraulics, throttle cracked . . . ." Klein read and I responded with the appropriate condition of each.

The Confederate Air Force's "Texas Raiders" is given a post-flight inspection.

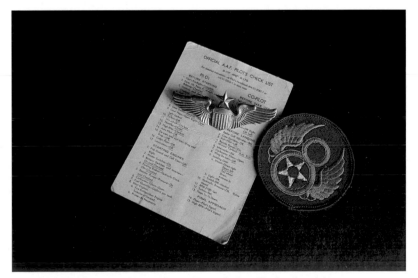

Original Army issue B-17F and G pilot's checklist.

Starting the engines required some teamwork. When the boost pump was on and its pressure noted, Klein activated the starter switch for the number three engine and counted nine blades of rotation. I selected the magneto switch to the BOTH position and watched for the telltale smoke around the cowl. Each of the cylinders began to fire and Klein eased the mixture lever to the AUTO-LEAN position, and toggled the primer switch, while keeping an eye on engine rpm. In this manner, we started each of the remaining three engines.

After a warm-up period, Muszala joined us in the cockpit, taking his seat as copilot. We performed engine runup, checked propellers, magnetos and all temps and pressures. Muszala briefed me on emergency procedures if we should have an engine failure on takeoff. Klein stood between us to monitor things, while Muszala explained the takeoff procedure. We were ready to fly.

I released the red parking brake lever and the bomber rolled forward without any throttle, running only on its idle rpm. As the plane eased forward, the tail wheel was unlocked so it could free-caster. To steer the bomber, I carefully applied the wheel brakes in the desired direction. I used outboard engine thrust to help initiate a turn, and to stop the turn, I used the opposite throttle. My taxi technique could in no way be described as smooth — the wheel brakes were sensitive and we more or less jerked and bumped our way through a series of zigzags out to the runway.

Checklist items completed, and tail wheel locked, I lined up on the runway ready for takeoff. Muszala told me to hold the brakes and advance the throttles to 30 inches manifold pressure. This accomplished, he gave me the thumbs up and I pushed the throttles forward and simultaneously released the brakes. The Boeing lunged forward, somewhat spiritedly, for a heavy bomber. We were light, however, by B-17 standards, carrying only five thousand pounds of fuel and a crew of three.

Once we were moving, I could steer with the rudder, but I slightly over-controlled with it: we veered left and right down the center line. I instinctively wanted to move the control wheel forward and lift the tail, but Muszala intervened, wanting me to let it fly off in slight tail low attitude, with almost neutral control position.

Accelerating through 100 miles per hour, the broad wings took hold and the bomber simply eased into the air. As the climb was established, I signaled to select the landing gear up and Muszala moved the electric switch. As I rolled the control wheel left to begin a gentle turn, I found I needed to adapt quickly to the heavy forces of the ailerons: the wheel felt like it was stuck. Using the distant horizon as an outside reference, I adjusted the pitch attitude for the climb and arrived quite close to the recommended 150 miles per hour.

Evergreen Venture's B-17G is joined in formation by the Confederate Air Force's "Sentimental Journey."

In the B-17's glazed nose section is the bombardier's
Norden bombsight.

"Rolling left, I observed the broad wings and engines;
the sluggish feel seemed appropriate to the mass being moved."

Muszala, our copilot, was at this point occupied with the first power reduction. I expected him to pull the throttles aft, but instead, he slowly dialed the electric supercharger control knob, reducing the amount of engine boost. The result was a gentle reduction in manifold pressure and a slight reduction of propeller rpm, with little noticeable change in the level of noise. I continued to climb and plied the controls trying to adapt to the sluggish feel and slow response. Rolling left, I observed the broad wing and engines; the sluggishness seemed appropriate to the mass being moved in the turn.

I considered the formidable task of bomber pilots of World War II, holding the heavy bomber in close formation. As the B-17s ventured deep into Europe, their close formation provided a concentrated defensive fire against German fighters. How demanding it must have been, especially at high altitudes, where the control response must have been worse.

Upon reaching six thousand feet, my job was to level off the big slug and try to maintain this altitude. I chased the swings of the altimeter some, while copilot Muszala deftly adjusted the throttles and propellers to cruise power. The cowl flaps were set to close, then locked. Stabilized, the airspeed indicated 170 miles per hour, for an "economical cruise," burning roughly two hundred gallons per hour.

In cruise, the noise subsided considerably. The sound of the four resonating engines slipping in and out of phase fit with my conceptions of the B-17 droning along. I rolled steeply to the left and established about forty-five degrees of bank to gain more feel of the controls. I checked our altitude, which had slowly slipped down to 5800 feet, and realized I needed to set the nose a little higher on the horizon. Because of its rock solid stability, nothing happens fast in the B-17; all changes in direction and altitude occur gradually. Left to its own devices, I believe this airplane would cruise without significant change in heading or altitude indefinitely.

STALL

To give me more of a feel for the slow-speed characteristics of the B-17, Muszala invited me to try a stall. I gradually reduced power, easing the throttles back. To slow the airplane, I used the pitch trim to hold the nose up, as the control pressure became heavy. When we had slowed to 140 miles per hour, we lowered the landing gear, and I observed the wheel emerging slowly from the number two engine nacelle. The flaps reached the "full down" position, and the speed bled off rapidly. As I eased the nose higher now, I noted that the elevator response was very much adequate. When our airspeed indicated 70 miles per hour, the control column began to shake and I felt some trembling in the right rudder pedal. As I pulled deeper into the stall, the controls trembled even more. There was no evident "break" left or right, just the shuddering or burbling air over the flight controls. When I relaxed my pull on the control wheel, the controls became smooth and the Fortress gradually began to accelerate. Muszala re-established the power to cruise, selected the gear to the UP position, and retracted the flaps incrementally. Surprisingly, the whole maneuver consumed only three hundred feet of altitude, and in the recovery, the bomber required no conscious effort to maintain altitude. The characteristics of the stall were much the same as the rest of airplane's personality — very stable, with gradual, incremental changes.

LANDING

As I turned for the airport, I rolled in some nose down trim and let the bomber pick up speed. In our descent, our speed increased to 200 miles per hour, demonstrating the inertia of the big Flying Fortress. As we entered the traffic pattern, we reduced the power to 20 inches manifold pressure, and gradually reduced speed as we flew parallel to the runway at about one thousand feet above the ground. When we had decelerated to about 140 miles per hour, I called for the landing gear and let the airplane continue to slow by holding altitude. To begin the descent, I banked gently toward the runway and let the nose come down. To slow to our target speed of 100 miles per hour, I extended the wing flaps in increments, making only minor changes in power. My greatest challenge was to establish the airplane on a straight track with the runway center line: at 110 miles per hour, the bomber was even more sluggish and difficult to maneuver.

Eventually, I lined up with the center line, slowing to the desired 100 miles per hour, as we crossed the end of the runway. The bomber's broad wings gave up lift gradually, demanding the throttles be brought to the idle position. I transitioned to flare, when Muszala discovered engines two and three still slightly above idle power, and pulled back on the levers. The bomber floated with excess speed for another five hundred feet or so, and quit flying just before I completed the flare to a three-point attitude. We hit the runway firmly and bounced back into the air: a bounce in a big airplane is something to reckon with, especially a 40,000-pound tail dragger. I stayed with the flight controls, dampening the second impact with gentle back pressure,

View from the ball turret, approaching the touchdown zone of the runway.

and regained control of the situation. I eased the tail down and continued to track the center line with full rudder inputs in alternating directions.

As we neared the end of the runway, I very gently applied the brakes and slowed the bomber to taxi speed. Klein called to unlock the tail wheel to allow for the runway turnoff. I exhaled slowly, concentrating on keeping the wheels on the pavement.

To pilot a B-17 for the first time was humbling. I thought of how challenging such a landing would be after having completed an exhausting eight-hour combat mission. Certainly a hundred hours or so of training in the airplane would develop a good feel, but I couldn't help but think of the nineteen-year-old pilot bringing nine crew members home in this machine with one, maybe two engines out, and unknown structural damage to the ship. No doubt about it, this was a highlight in my experience, having tried my hand at one of the legends of aviation history.

Looking Back

To fly these legends of aviation has provided me with more than just a unique entry in the logbook — it was a realized ambition. My few days as a pseudo-cadet helped me to make a special kind of connection with these historic aircraft, to come to realize their individual personalities: the charm and balance of the Stearman, the stubborn handling of the Texan, the horsepower and maneuverability of the Mustang, and the seemingly ever-steady stability of the Flying Fortress — these are things I will never forget. Furthermore, to fly with expert flight instructors of these machines — like Glenn MacDonald who trained during the war — has provided an added dimension to my understanding of this turbulent, yet innovative, time in world history.

Today, we cross the states in a matter of hours, cruising in complacent comfort, and perhaps taking our luxury for granted. When we look back about fifty years, even under the best of circumstances, a pilot struggled with 200 miles per hour cruise speeds in freezing temperatures. At that time, the tail wheel represented the leading edge of technology for steering; the pilot had a challenge just keeping the airplane moving straight across the ground. After working within the limited technologies of fifty years past, I was confronted, in a concrete way, with my perhaps facile conceptions stemming from my childhood fascination with military aircraft. Although flying these classic airplanes has tempered my quixotic ideas about the first decades of aviation, these experiences — adapting to the equipment and conditions of each airplane — have not curbed my enthusiasm for their technology. I have, rather, increased my appreciation for the evolutionary changes in aviation over the past fifty years.

After many years of marveling at these machines, I had an intense anticipation when I finally did occupy the cockpit. Gaining an understanding of the necessary skills and techniques, I felt a much greater appreciation for those who flew these machines when they were the best there was.

Nose art carries on the colorful wartime tradition.

The North Dakota sunset reflects on the wings of a newly restored Grumman TBM-3E torpedo bomber.

CHAPTER 2

Restoring the Best of the Past

Keep 'em Flying

To restore means to repair, replace, rejuvenate, revitalize; the synonyms are numerous and interpretation of the term is loose. Many times restorers don't know where to begin. The decisions are many: whether to add or subtract components, or simply re-create the original item. Sometimes the airplane is restored with what an informed World War II historian might consider good taste, true to its historical nature; other times a plane is restored to what the same palate might consider ostentatious, or even ridiculous. In some instances, an airplane is not simply restored, but rebuilt and customized. The plane receives polish, chrome, electronics and instrumentation that the designer and manufacturer had never imagined. These airplanes are no longer warplanes; their roles now reflect their contemporary owners.

The decisions made by each particular restorer may offend some, yet delight others. These are the decisions of the artist and remain for the rest of us to simply interpret. As in any artwork, the beauty is in the eyes of the beholder. But however a plane is restored, it is the mere fact that a fifty-year-old piece of machinery can still take to the air that is impressive.

AIR SHOWS AND ENTHUSIASTS

At an air show, the airplanes don't just look good. They aren't merely preserved as museum showpieces — these planes perform! You realize their combustive vitality, experientially, when you hear the first muffled eruptions of exhaust and feel the air rushing from the propellers, spinning vigorously, gaining momentum, and culminating in a throbbing asynchronous rumble. In a procession, the planes emerge, weaving right and left, raising a cloud of dust and grass in their wake. The rumble of their engines increases to a thunderous roar, and two of the winged beasts bolt forth from the pack. In pairs, the others follow suit and, in a show of grace and power, the show has begun.

The tremendous noise that accompanies every air show is part of the experience. But to an air enthusiast like me, and I imagine to most fans of aeronautica, the most vivid and essential ingredient of the air show are the *Warbirds*. For these aeronautical thoroughbreds alone, many people come to the aerial demonstrations. But the number of warplanes that we find at a typical air show has not always played such a significant part — their presence at the event is a relatively recent phenomenon. Through a worldwide dedication of individuals and organizations, there has been a dramatic resurgence in the number of Warbirds. In the 1950s few people purchased and restored a derelict or neglected airplane with the intent of *preserving aviation heritage*. Before the end of that decade, however, more organized efforts saved some of the classic airplanes which were fast disappearing from existence. Of particular note, in this respect, was the official organization of The Confederate Air Force (CAF). The efforts of this group, more than any other, has heightened public interest in the survival of World War II combat aircraft.

From its humble beginnings in 1957, located in the lower Rio Grande Valley of Texas, the CAF has grown to include participants not only in the United States, but many other countries as well. Their self-assigned task is to preserve and fly at least one example of each American combat aircraft of the Second World War. Success in that assignment has also fostered the collection and restoration of many foreign types of aircraft. At the annual American Air Power Demonstration, at the CAF's Midland, Texas, headquarters, thousands of people witness each October the unique sight and sound of these remarkable aircraft as they take to the air.

Since the 1960s a growing number of privately funded organizations have collected, restored and flown the classic warbirds which are displayed at air show events around the country. Since the late 1970s and early 1980s, the trend has considerably increased in momentum, with the establishment of more elaborate display facilities and annual flight demonstration events.

From individual aircraft owners to the largest private collections, there has been a whirlwind of effort to "keep 'em flying." The Experimental Aircraft Association, the largest single group of aviation enthusiasts in the world, has established a special subculture of their organization, Warbirds of America. Composed of thousands of individual aircraft owners, pilots and supporters, the group brings together an enormous gathering of classic military aircraft each August at the EAA's annual convention in Oshkosh, Wisconsin.

The general resurgence in the population of the once nearly extinct warbirds continues be to made possible through the tireless efforts of aircraft mechanics and

restoration specialists, who dedicate years of labor to their individual projects. The facilities range from commercial operations, working with multiple customers, to individual owners in small airport hangars, but the theme is invariably the same: a commitment to keeping the classic aircraft flying.

For some aviation enthusiasts, restoring a classic airplane has become virtually an obsession. On the outskirts of almost any town, a typical scene takes place: a sleepy country airport and a small hangar, its spaces crammed with the remnants of a dismantled biplane. Its skeletal wooden wings hang from the walls, devoid of fabric covering, while two men, for the moment oblivious to their obligations at home, work persistently on the cage-like structure of a fuselage. The mingling fumes of aviation gasoline, butyrate, and nitrate dopes permeate the musty space.

To these two laboring men, this smell is the scent of heaven. The older of the men, a cabinet maker by trade, repairs a cracked wing-tip bow and replaces deteriorated ribs. Spread before him are some pieces of spruce, a bottle of wood glue and a few handfuls of tacking nails. His partner, an electrician, is busy with his rib stitching. He is newly married; his wife has already began to complain about his growing preoccupation with the plane. The older man, a veteran at this restoring passion, knows his wife has adapted to the inconveniences of his consuming avocation.

Both men, like their counterparts around the country, have invested a small fortune and countless hours into this airplane. Yet, for a few more years, as each piece of hardware is meticulously selected and adjusted to perfection, they can only console themselves with their vision of the finished work: piloting the mint condition Boeing, with the open cockpit, the wind, and the whistle of the flying wires to tantalize their senses. As their weekends, evenings and holidays melt into years toward the project's anticipated completion, they sustain their stamina with this vision of the future. In such hangars as this — a place an untrained observer may describe as uneventful — aero-technology of the 1920s, and the associated skills of rib stitching and fabric doping, are being preserved and perpetuated.

TRI-STATE AVIATION

At a rural airport, in a larger hangar than our imaginary "typical" restoration site, we find a familiar theme — obsessed warbird fanatics busily at work — but here there is a different tempo. The pace is quicker and the hands are busier.

This particular shop — Tri-State Aviation, in North Dakota — is, as far as restoration facilities go, unconventional. Although the contagious enthusiasm, the

A vision of the future: the completed project.

Craftsmen work the soft aluminum parts
with measured precision.

meticulous attention and historical ambiance are all familiar, there is something else happening here. Tri-State Aviation is carrying on a tradition that goes beyond the endeavors of the typical restoration facility: it actually manufactures new parts, and not just for one plane at a time, but for multiples of ten! The walls are lined with bins of newly formed parts arranged in a neat, categorical fashion. In another room, we see a new fuselage taking shape. Again, this is not a rebuilt fuselage, but one made entirely of new parts, the beginnings of a brand new P-51 Mustang. The Tri-State staff develops all the tooling necessary for each part, according to the specifications of North American Aviation engineering drawings. Although Tri-State's manufacturing techniques are rudimentary compared to those of the Inglewood, California, plant of 1944, the methods serve them well, nonetheless.

Assorted tools for metalwork squeal, screech or shriek, depending on their task, as they mold sheet metal into various shapes — familiar shapes that make up an airplane's exterior surface or structure. Over on the far end of the hangar, a hydraulic press howls, exerting thousands of pounds of pressure to form an aluminum encasement for a wing. Two craftsmen, working with the determination of Renaissance architects, manipulate its soft metal with measured precision. In an adjoining room, a technician examines microfilms for structural detail and dimension. One closed-in area, looking rather temporary, serves as an office, where the proprietor, a phone curled around his face, is engaged in negotiations for parts. He is perhaps haggling over prices, discussing an inventory of parts to be auctioned in Florida, or negotiating a trade for propeller hubs somewhere in Canada. Here, time, skill and resourcefulness are the most valued assets, and sometimes, the largest obstacles.

Gerald Beck's Tri-State Aviation is a thriving North Dakota crop spraying business. The small machine shop in the back of the hangar, however, has been transformed into a small production facility. Beck's first project was a Chance-Vought Corsair. The nearly completed fighter stands as testament to his experience in aircraft recovery and restoration. Later he bought a Grumman TBM Avenger which had been retired from crop spraying in Canada. "I needed bomb bay doors," he recalls, gesturing toward the torpedo bomber, "but I couldn't find a serviceable set." After some investigation of the Grumman drawings, Beck decided to attempt building a set of doors. The cost of the equipment and tooling for such a project would be the same, he reasoned, whether he built one set or ten. So he built ten. Eight of the ten sets were sold to other rebuilders, and thus began a new subsidiary business for Tri-State — in parts manufacture.

Goodyear FG-1D cockpit: before restoration.

P-51D Mustang cockpit: after restoration.

Soon afterward, work began on two Mustang projects. Beck and friend Bob Odegaard each had an interest in rebuilding a P-51 and had begun to search for the requisite pieces. Wings, tail members, engine — the parts were forthcoming, but many from crashed airplanes, mostly bent and of dubious value. As the search continued, Odegaard says, "I found two right wings in Switzerland which had survived some sort of target practice." He received the right wings but was unable to locate matching left wings. Odegaard had no choice but to build them from scratch. His developing skill brought forth customers with two sets of P-51 wings for remanufacture.

Thus an interesting relationship has developed: Beck specializes in work on the fuselage while nearby, in a separate facility, Odegaard concentrates on the wings. Naturally, my first inclination was to ask, "How many orders for new Mustangs?" Both were quick to emphasize that their interest is not in building P-51 clones. While it appears to be entirely within their reach to assemble a new airframe, this is not the purpose of their work. Their individual projects prompted the manufacture of many new parts, and subsequently, a demand has developed for their specialized talents.

To rebuild fuselages for customers, Beck had accumulated an extensive inventory of fuselage parts. At the time of my visit, he had constructed a fuselage of "eighty to ninety percent" new parts. The present customer had provided a complete wing, but very little of the fuselage. Odegaard observes, "The days of strip and paint restoration are long gone." The rebuilder faces extensive parts fabrication and, generally speaking, the airplane is built of parts from any number of sources. As the search for parts becomes less fruitful, the fabrication of parts becomes the likelier option.

These two men have pursued their interest in rebuilding the Mustang into what appears to be a marketable commodity. In addition to supplying the needs of their own projects, they are able to supply other rebuilders with a nearly complete selection of structural parts, or assemblies made up from those parts. Previously, a customer could wait up to two years for a specialist to handcraft a single assembly. Though a growing number of maintenance facilities are specializing in rebuilding the fighters and bombers, no others have dedicated their efforts to relieving the parts shortage.

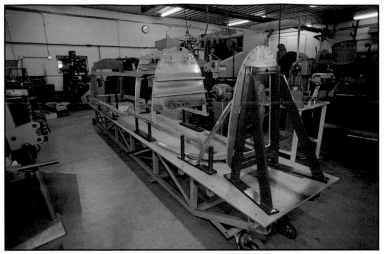

Mustang's fuselage front frame section being built on jig.

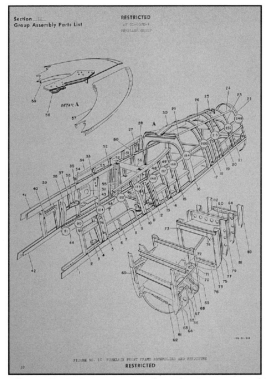

Page from P-51D parts catalog depicts assembly
of parts in the Mustang's fuselage.

Completed front frame and tail cone: built of
approximately 85 percent new parts.

Laid out in pieces, the P-51 bore little resemblance to the powerhouse I had flown during my brief adventure in advanced fighter training. The Mustang's fuselage is composed of four sections which are built separately, then joined together: the fuselage front section, the radiator intake duct, the tail cone and the engine mount structure. Beck first attempted to replicate the radiator intake duct, which forms the airplane's distinctive belly scoop. This assembly is now in demand among rebuilders, since the supply of available spares has been largely consumed over the years by landing accidents. So, when a customer provided Beck with a poorly rebuilt intake duct for repair, he decided that it might be easier to just build a new one. Each component part was cut and formed to specification and marked with the North American part number for standardization. A special jig was built to maintain proper positioning and alignment of parts during assembly. The jig is a steel frame, accurately marked with reference lines, called stations, which determine the location of each part. The structural repair manual provides a station mapping for the entire airframe. Subsequently, similar tooling and jigs were developed for the tail cone and front fuselage sections, followed by production of ten sets of parts for each. Beck contends that a properly built assembly should fit onto any Mustang without modification. The unique engine mount structure is being examined for future production; however, spares are still relatively available, which limits the marketability of new replacements.

The front fuselage section is the largest section and is the main body to which the wings, tail cone, and radiator intake duct are mounted. The structure is supported by four longerons which are solid alloy extrusions. The original extrusions were made of an alloy with a high magnesium content, which made them susceptible to corrosion. For this reason, several P-51s have undergone restoration to replace these members. An independent manufacturer has been making the longerons for several years and supplies them for Beck's projects. These are made of a newer, more corrosion resistant alloy, which more or less eliminates this problem. The bulkheads and framework which surround the longerons are formed from aluminum sheet stock using a hydraulic press. The framework of longerons, bulkheads, formers and stringers is then assembled on the jig.

The structure is completed with the application of skins over the framework. Creative solutions were developed to form the skins of compound curvature in a cost effective and repeatable fashion. A duplicate of the upper fuselage was cast in rein-

Interior of "new" Mustang fuselage
displays protective coatings applied to metal.

Hydraulic press used to form
aluminum structural parts.

Assorted original North American made Mustang parts
come from all manner of sources.

forced concrete, over which the heavy sheet aluminum is "stretched" to the desired shape. Beck emphasizes that these techniques are not new, but simply and effectively adapted to the task at an appropriate cost. Flush riveting of the skins to the framework is an art form unto itself. Each rivet hole must be countersunk to match the rivet head's tapered shape, so the skin can be fastened to the frame with a smooth surface. The riveter's skill is mirrored in the finish of the airplane's polished skin.

The measure of accuracy built into the completed fuselage is apparent in the fit of the canopy. A North American made windshield frame and canopy were fitted to the structure without need of adjustment. The canopy rolls smoothly on its rails, without binding, and closes with a flush alignment of its edges to the fuselage skin contour. It simply fits.

MUSTANG WINGS

In Kindred, North Dakota, population six hundred, is Bob Odegaard's shop: a shop which is almost entirely dedicated to constructing wings.

The wings are a more complex undertaking than the fuselage. The perimeter of the hangar hosts a collection of metal forming, cutting and bending equipment. On the wall, a variety of scavenged Mustang parts share space with shiny, newly-made wing ribs and spars. In the center of the floor, mounted on steel supports, rest two sets of wings under reconstruction. Five craftsmen are busy with individual projects, including the development of new parts tooling and remanufacturing of wing parts. Odegaard supervises each project with his meticulous eye for quality and detail.

Long considered one of aviation's most artistic creations, the P-51 is a combination of compound curves and low drag aerodynamics. The design process was one of the first to employ a computer to minimize drag. The wing's airfoil section used the newly developed "laminar flow" technology, which also improved drag characteristics, especially at high speed. These features not only contributed to the fighter's superior performance, but also to the complexity of its construction. The two sets of wings under restoration have revealed some interesting information about wartime production standards. Parts removed from these wings show noticeable differences from the dimensions specified in the engineering drawings. Joining of skin panels also shows measurable variation between the two sets of wings. Apparently, the demand for combat aircraft necessitated some latitude in quality control to assure expected production rates. Areas of corrosion in the fuel cell cavities and machine

Jig used to assemble ribs and spar members with correct position and alignment.

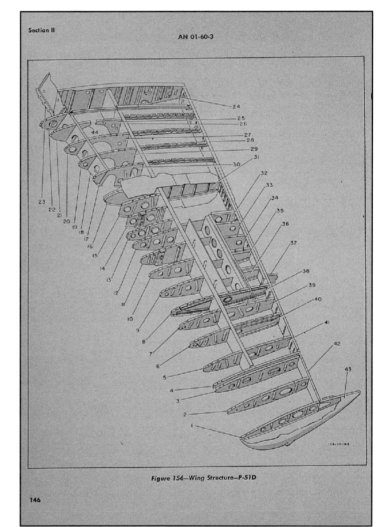

A page from the P-51D structural repair manual shows arrangement of ribs, formers and spar members in Mustang wing.

gun bays, demonstrate the lack of protective primer coatings afforded to a combat aircraft whose life expectancy was measured in weeks, instead of years.

The new parts being fabricated have resulted from many hours of design and preparation of accurate cutting patterns and press blocks. Odegaard presses the wing ribs to shape in a hydraulic press of his own design. Built from equipment available in his shop, it exerts up to five hundred tons per square inch to form the ribs to an exacting standard. Each rib is unique, which has mandated the time-consuming development of individual sets of patterns. The large main spar requires multiple bends to produce the desired taper in the wing's thickness from root to tip.

Many of the procedures being used are the result of much trial and error. Several of the wing's structural components are of compound curvature, which further complicated the methods to be used in forming the metal. The shaping of the former strips, which span the wing's fuel cell cavities, proved particularly challenging, since they provide for both the wing's upper surface curvature and support. Another source of pride for Odegaard are the machine gun blisters in the wing's leading edge.

Wing from a rare P-51C under restoration at Odegaard's Kindred, North Dakota, shop.

"We benefited from our failures," he comments, "because each attempt adds to your understanding of the material and methods."

Many valuable lessons have been learned on the two wing restoration projects, which will help make things easier when assembling the new wing structures. Rivets must be bucked into tight and uncompromising locations. The sheer volume of flush fitting rivets in the wing is intimidating. Again, the structural repair manual provides some illustrative insight into these problems, but none like the actual practice.

A main jig assembly stands ready in one corner of the facility, with a spar and some ribs already in place. Another smaller jig was built expressly for the purpose of shaping the three leading edge skins. The fit of the leading edge skin determines the camber of the wing and, hence, the performance of the wing. The jig also allows for the precise location of holes for the rivets which secure the skins. The techniques being employed are devised specifically for each part or assembly, for precise, consistent results. While each assembly is essentially being handmade, each successive attempt improves tolerances and requires less time.

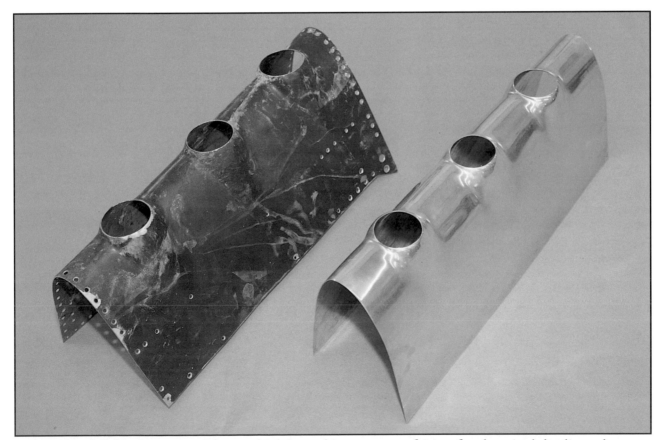

Original (left) compares with new (right) machine gun port fairing for the wing's leading edge.

Lone Star Flight Museum's Grumman F6F Hellcat and
FM-2 Wildcat join formation over Galveston, Texas.

Once they have completed the parts tooling and finalized the assembly techniques, they can begin assembling the matching left wing for Odegaard's airplane. The success of this endeavor will be measured in several respects. For two men in North Dakota, it will be the completion of their airplanes, and successful flight tests. For others who fly "vintage" aircraft into the next century, the resources expended by these two men in the development of tooling and parts manufacture, will help to ensure that Mustangs continue to fly.

Flying Museums

Around the United States, private owners dedicated to restoring old airplanes to flying condition have helped to establish "flying museums." These collections represent substantial private investments in aircraft, display facilities, maintenance and operations. To offset the costs of the operation, fees for membership are required to provide additional income. Supplementing a paid full-time staff, volunteers donate their time, skills and assistance that is required to host the annual display events. Staff pilots are volunteers, selected for their experience and availability, as it suits the particular operation of the organization.

LONE STAR FLIGHT MUSEUM

The Lone Star Flight Museum of Galveston, Texas, is an excellent example of the modern flying museum. Established as a private collection in 1985, the need for a dedicated display facility was immediately apparent. Five years later, in November of 1990, the new facility opened, boasting over forty aircraft and sixty thousand square feet of temperature and humidity controlled display space, establishing a new standard of excellence.

Director Jim Fausz, having successfully established the Champlin Fighter Museum in Mesa, Arizona, was recruited to build the new Lone Star Museum in 1985. Fausz helped the museum with its first major step: providing an appropriate home for the aircraft. By 1990, the museum decided to establish a general membership, and to help with this endeavor, they recruited former Confederate Air Force executive director, Ralph Royce. Today one thousand strong, members provide continuing financial support for the organization's operations and growth, and additionally, these members volunteer manpower for maintenance and display events.

Another of Lone Star Flight Museum's collection of famous Grumman Cats, the F7F-3 Tigercat.

Lone Star's B-17G carries the authentic markings of the 303rd
Heavy Bomb Group's "Thunderbird."

As visitors enter Lone Star's spacious display hangars, the mood is set by the pervading theme of Glenn Miller's "American Patrol." The surrounding artifacts and memorabilia give the uninitiated a true feeling of a different era in time. The 303rd Heavy Bomb group's B-17G Flying Fortress, *Thunderbird*, is authentically rendered in its original Eighth Air Force colors. Adjacent to the heavy bomber is its single engine companion or "little friend," Republic P-47G Thunderbolt. The names go on, in a seemingly endless string . . . *Havoc, Hellcat . . . Lightning, Lodestar . . . Catalina, Corsair . . . Tigercat, Texan . . . Wildcat, Warhawk . . . Harvard, Harpoon . . .* each name represented by one of the finest existing examples of that historic aircraft.

Lone Star Flight Museum features a magnificent static display of aircraft, one of the largest private collections in the world. The planes, however, remain static only temporarily; the purpose of the museum is to have each plane operationally prepared for flight. The technical staff is responsible for the operational readiness of their fleet, according to the demands of the annual air show bookings. A seasonal rotation selects certain aircraft for licensing and air show duty. The museum typically can field over a half dozen fighters and bombers for a regional event, providing a dazzling display of air power.

Lone Star pilot, Mike Burke, on a sweep of Galveston Bay in the P-40E Kittyhawk.

Lone Star's graceful Lockheed P-38L Lightning over Breckenridge, Texas.

Cockpit of the unique Lockheed Lightning.

At 2200 feet above sea level, southern Arizona's Avra Valley presents some striking contrasts. Ringed by steeply rising red rock outcroppings, the vast expanses of Sonoran desert support a lush flora of sage scrub, wild flowers and cacti. The towering saguaro symbolize the unique character of this land. An intense summer monsoon season offsets the normally dry climate with a theatrical display of lightning and thunder, unrivaled anywhere in the continental United States.

In 1944 this was the site of Army Air Force's advanced flight training school, Marana AAF. Fleets of polished North American AT-6s ranged the desert skies in pursuit of gunnery, navigations and formation flying skills. The dry climate and clear air ideally suited the Army's task. Today, the site provides a similar function: the Marana facility is operated by Evergreen International Airlines, Inc., for the heavy maintenance and inspections of their Boeing 747 fleet.

A few vestiges of Marana's past still remain as a reminder of that time: the field's triangle runways, arched hangars and the original control tower are evidence of the Army's former presence. In stark contrast to the jumbo jetliners, a small fleet of vintage aircraft share the airport's concrete ramps and runways. The muffled cough of a starting radial engine still haunts the high desert: it is not a ghost plane echoing the sound of a bygone era — rather, it is part of Evergreen International.

In a nearby hangar, craftsmen hear the commotion and know the sound all too well. They put down their tools, momentarily, to witness the awakening of the three remaining engines, taking a small measure of satisfaction in the event. Within minutes, the sound builds to a mighty crescendo, as the engines reach their maximum

Evergreen Ventures' majestic B-17G reflects the deep blue sky in its highly polished aluminum finish.

power, tugging forward the 35,000-pound Boeing B-17. The liftoff is gradual, then the bomber arcs skyward, as the polished silver wings develop increasing lift, and gradually the plane and its synchronous sound fade away.

A division of Evergreen International Aviation, Evergreen Ventures is responsible for the restoration and maintenance of the B-17 and a host of other equally famous World War II era aircraft. The collection is being readied for a new aviation museum facility, being established at Evergreen's headquarters in McMinnville, Oregon. The centerpiece of this display will be the famed Hughes HK-1 flying boat, known as the *Spruce Goose*.

Inside one of Marana's vintage hangars, work continues on Evergreen's most notable project: the Lockheed P-38L Lightning, undergoing major reconstruction. Though the airplane was flown to Marana, its general condition was such that it required a thorough restoration program. Evergreen Ventures' Bill Muszala, who oversees the maintenance, restoration and flying of the Marana-based collection, gave me an overview of the project.

Extensive surface corrosion throughout the P-38's airframe has required complete disassembly. Its engines and wings, its stabilizer and tail booms had each been removed, as well as a myriad of hydraulic, electric and mechanical control systems. The remaining centerpiece, consisting of the inboard wing sections, center fuselage pod and forward boom sections, have been treated for corrosion.

To remove the corrosion, all interior and exterior surfaces had been stripped of paint and treated with an acid metal "brightener." Apparently, the airplane had previously been "rebuilt" and the corroded parts and sections had been simply "painted over" with primer. Muszala stresses the importance of the removal of the deteriorated metal, and its subsequent coating for long-term protection. "With corrosion," Muszala states, "it's pay me now, or pay me later. There's no way to avoid dealing with it." Virtually every part on the airplane is being treated individually, prior to reassembly.

Working on metal preparation was Louis Piergallini, who described to me his experiences with coating processes. Some modernization is being incorporated into the coatings to improve their longevity. Brightened surfaces are first treated with a conversion coating, to improve the adherence of paint. Instead of the original zinc chromate primer on interior surfaces, Muszala has specified the use of two-part epoxy primers and an additional coating of polyurethane paint, mixed to duplicate the yellow and green colors of the original zinc coatings. The exterior of the P-38 will feature a polished bare aluminum finish.

The plane was originally manufactured by Lockheed as a photo-reconnaissance version, with an extended camera nose. During the 1950s and early '60s, the reconnaissance version found a commercial utility role as an aerial mapping platform. This particular aircraft, with several other Lightnings, served this function for many years, and that is likely responsible for its survival to this date. The fighter nose had been refitted to the airplane at some point, but was somewhat precariously riveted in place, without respect to the proper structural considerations. With the aid of Lockheed drawings, Muszala directed that the nose be removed for rework and reinstallation. As the Evergreen mechanics began work on the aircraft, they discovered that other systems of the aircraft had been modified and adapted for commercial use, thus requiring that these systems be restored to their original standard configurations. The project was being completed with an exceptional degree of exacting research and detailed workmanship, which characterizes all of the work performed at the Evergreen facility.

Evergreen P-38L before arrival at Marana facility.

Removal and repair of P-38's fighter nose.

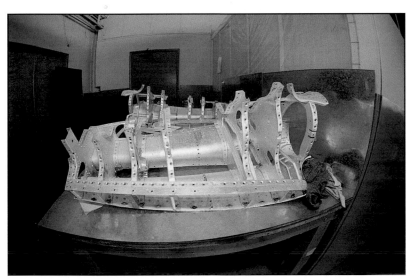

Freshly acid-etched structure prior to primer coating.

Left boom section displays degree of disassembly and
protective coating applied to internal structures.

Evergreen's collection includes several of the most famous World War II fighters. On my visit I noticed, in particular, a rare Curtiss P-40K Warhawk, a Goodyear-built FG1-D Corsair, and a highly polished North American P-51D Mustang. Under restoration by specialist Daryl Skurich in Fort Collins, Colorado, are a pair of Messerschmitt Bf 109s. These extremely rare aircraft were located in Czechoslovakia and will fly with the original Daimler-Benz DB 605 engine.

Perhaps the most significant aircraft maintained and flown by Evergreen is the Boeing B-17G Flying Fortress. Operated by Evergreen in several utility roles, the bomber last saw service as a fire bomber before being restored to its present configuration. The interior of the B-17 has been faithfully restored with all the original crew stations and equipment. The bomber's defensive machine gun turrets, including a functional ball turret on the belly, have also been refitted to original configuration. The highly polished Flying Fortress is flown on an extensive tour of events each season, highlighting the Evergreen collection.

The Marana-based aircraft will be transferred to McMinnville, following completion of the *Spruce Goose* restoration, and the construction of the large museum structure around the giant flying boat. The flyable aircraft will enjoy a protected environment for public display, and will also be available for air show and demonstration flying. Evergreen's dedication to the preservation of historic aircraft will expose the sight and sound of aviation's past to yet a broader audience in the Pacific Northwest.

As the popularity of these large flying museums like Lone Star and Evergreen International has soared in the past decade, so has the size of each collection. In addition to providing a "healthy" operating environment for the airplanes, the organization brings together the interests of the community with the skill and knowledge of dedicated professionals. Progressive maintenance and professionally trained flight crews help to ensure the longterm survival of many of the rarest examples of these aircraft.

Taking Flight

Brought back to life, the colorful warbirds soar again in their natural element: the Messerschmitt 109; its arch nemesis, the Supermarine Spitfire; and the Mitsubishi Zero — now older than their pilots, in many cases, yet still hearty and graceful in flight. Making their gradual return from near extinction, these rare survivors are examples of some of the most feared and famous fighters of their time. The only thrill

Evergreen Ventures' Mike Smith poses their Goodyear FG-1D Corsair "Ruthless II."

Cockpit of FG-1D Corsair.

greater than seeing these machines in motion is, perhaps, taking the pilot's seat and experiencing the nearly lost secrets of flight these airplanes hold. Some of the pilots who have been fortunate enough to fly these aircraft have shared their impressions of that unique experience.

MESSERSCHMITT

"Looking down into the tiny space I was about to occupy, I grinned nervously, trying to decide how I might slip in gracefully. Climbing over the edge, and stepping in the seat, I turned a little sideways and slid down in position. Sitting on the floor, semi-reclined, my legs stretched slightly upward to reach the rudder pedals. With the flat-paned, heavy structure of the canopy closed over my head, the feeling was complete. Caged! I forced my attention to the more immediate surroundings. Feeling the grasp of the throttle and control stick, and reaching for the landing gear lever, the arrangement was one of utility, with controls and indicators at my fingertips. On the floor between my feet was a platform, now empty, where the 20mm cannon breech had once been. It was placed here so that the pilot could fire the weapon through the propeller shaft with lethal accuracy. I could only imagine the sound and reflex of an artillery piece being fired as I straddled it. This was not a comfortable place to work, I thought, shifting my gaze to the lattice of bars surrounding my head.

"Preparation for my first flight, especially the takeoff and landing, included a good deal of study, as I was well aware of the Messerschmitt's reputation for poor ground handling. The takeoff was actually sort of anticlimactic, since I really anticipated the worst. Though the plane's rudder is quite small, it is easily adequate, for the control of engine torque during the takeoff. The narrow track of the landing gear, and the inadequate mechanical drum brakes, make directional control difficult at best on landing. The tail wheel is not steerable, and remains locked during the landing, so a three-point, or full stall landing had been recommended to me by several pilots with experience in this airplane, to reduce the tendency to swerve after touchdown. On some landings, the plane just rolls straight ahead . . . but you can't relax your guard until you've stopped it."

— *Messerschmitt pilot, Kent Sherman*

Workplace of the Messerschmitt pilot: utilitarian.

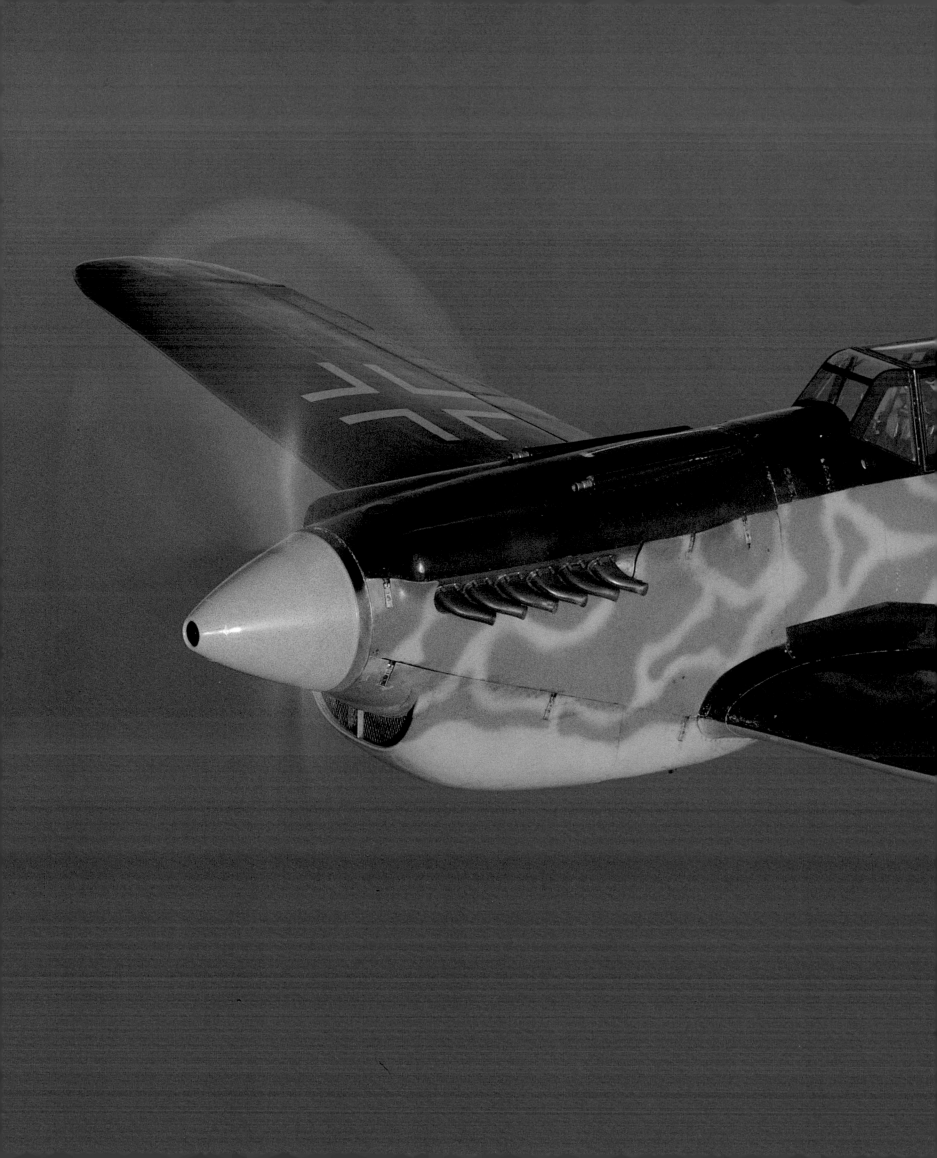

Tight confines of the Spitfire Mk XVI cockpit.

"The beautiful lines of the Spitfire allow little excess space for the pilot. To permit entry into the narrow cockpit, a side hatch in the fuselage opens to the left of the seat. Once seated, with the hatch secured, the canopy rails fit snugly with the pilot's shoulders. By comparison with American fighters, the Spitfire is truly 'strapped on' before flight. From a 'foreign' pilot's point of view, the British fighter incorporates a few differences evident in the instrumentation and controls. On the forward panel, the engine's primary power gauge is marked BOOST. The top of the stick features a circular 'spade grip,' which pivots laterally at the top of the column to effect roll control. Located on the grip is a lever which controls air pressure to the wheel brakes. Pneumatic pressure is provided by a small pump mounted on the Merlin engine's accessory section, and it is also used to extend the wing flaps and operate the radiator exit flaps.

"The Spitfire's ground handling is actually quite user friendly. The pneumatic brakes, being applied in conjunction with the rudder pedals, simply require a squeeze on the control lever to effect a sharper turn on the ground. In a crosswind takeoff or landing, with full rudder applied, a simple squeeze on the brake lever accommodates any additional directional control needed.

"To raise the landing gear after takeoff, the pilot must switch the left hand to the control grip and use the right hand to hold the gear lever in the up position, until it is retracted. It's very important to check the throttle's friction lock before switching hands, to avoid an embarrassing power failure right after takeoff. I learned this little secret of the Spitfire from personal experience!

"Once airborne, the controls feel light and responsive, with no undesirable flight characteristics. If you pull too hard on the stick, the airplane just sort of shakes and shudders — like it's trying to tell you something — without tendency to snap roll in the stall."

— *Spitfire pilot, Bud Granley*

The Messerschmitt's lines resemble those of
a shark, ready to slash at its prey.

Bud Granley shows the Spitfire's classic elliptical
planform wing to advantage.

"The Mitsubishi Zero is a piece of history, and I feel very fortunate to have had the opportunity to have touched that piece of history. The airplane suffered a long and somewhat arduous journey back to life, coming out of the jungles of the Soloman Islands in the Southwest Pacific, through recovery to Canada, and later to Harlingen, Texas, in the possession of the Confederate Air Force. The restoration took approximately three years, and tens of thousands of volunteer hours, utilizing the expertise of the National Air and Space Museum to detail it accurately. The Zero is a dream to fly, especially in air show demonstrations against American fighters like the Warhawk or Wildcat, since they simply cannot maneuver or climb with it. The later American fighters, like the Mustang or Corsair, however, compete well in such a contest against the Zero.

"The takeoff and climb are the most challenging aspect of flying the Zero. Once off the ground, the fighter must be pulled up very steeply, to allow for the retraction of the landing gear. At airspeeds of more than 105 knots, the hydraulic system simply cannot retract the wheels into the wells. While performing this maneuver, the left hand is switched from the throttle to the control stick, and the right hand from the stick to a lever behind the right shoulder, to begin the gear retraction cycle. When the gear indicates in the UP position, a forward nudge on the stick provides a slight negative G, to hold the wheels in position while the lever is again moved to engage the uplocks. From my experience with the Zero, I gained much admiration for Japanese pilots who performed this complicated procedure while taking off in formation.

"When the landing gear retraction exercise is completed, you put the nose down and accelerate to about 135 knots, where the Zero climbs out at 3500 feet per minute. The fighter has large aileron surfaces, which gives it a very crisp roll rate. At speeds above 240 knots, however, the controls become very rigid — above 275 knots the airplane is virtually impossible to maneuver with any dexterity. Landings are typical for a tail wheel type airplane, with forward visibility being very poor at approach speeds below 90 knots. I use about 95 knots, and make the approach steep enough to be able to see the runway over the nose."

— *Confederate Air Force Sponsor and Zero pilot, John Kelley*

Confederate Air Force's John Kelley poses the Mitsubishi A6M2 Zero.

CHAPTER 3

Preserving the Best of the Past

On public display at the National Air and Space Museum in Washington, D.C., brandishing a black swastika on its tail fin, is a rare technological milestone in aviation, the Messerschmitt Me 262. The sleek German design was the world's first operational jet fighter. Rushed through development, the fighter's jet engines were capable of only ten hours of operation. After that, they required a complete overhaul.

The Me 262 at the National Air and Space Museum (NASM) is so well preserved that a museum visitor could easily take both its existence and condition for granted. One might assume that after World War II, such airplanes were simply transported from the base to the museum, polished, detailed and then displayed. This is, however, far from the truth. The existence of these aircraft is the result of years of research, refurbishment, and a little luck. Many of the airplanes, like the Me 262, were saved on the brink of extinction: after the war, most aircraft were simply disassembled and destroyed.

Ironically, in 1946 the U.S. government sanctioned the idea of preserving historically significant aircraft at a time when the U.S. military was destroying, wholesale, vast fleets of warplanes for use as scrap metal. Shortly after the war, the Army Air Force's commanding general Henry "Hap" Arnold successfully convinced congressional leaders that it was a national interest to permanently preserve and store one example of each type aircraft of World War II. Captured Japanese and German warplanes formed the nucleus of what is now the National Air and Space Museum collection in Washington, D.C.

Prior to this campaign, Paul E. Garber had collected historically significant aircraft as part of the Smithsonian Institution's History and Technology collection. The collection subsequently included examples of both civilian models and U.S. Army and Navy aircraft, many being retired from active service. Today, this collection resides primarily at the Paul E. Garber facility in Suitland, Maryland, just outside of Washington, D.C. As the name implies, Mr. Garber was instrumental in the establishment of this facility for the safekeeping of the collection's many valuable artifacts.

One of the amazing aspects of the National Air and Space Museum in Washington is its ability to perpetually display new and different exhibits. These ever-changing displays are a reflection of the museum's vast collection of aircraft. Limited space permits only a fraction of the available collection to be displayed for the public. Aircraft are continuously being rotated from storage to display, and back to storage; several aircraft have been loaned for the long term to aviation museums around the world. The largest part of the collection is not in Washington, but remains in storage where the collection first began at NASM's Garber facility. Here, a staff of dedicated craftsmen perform exacting preservation and restoration work. Its warehouses store hundreds of airplanes, some disassembled, others intact, remaining in the condition in which they arrived. A tour of the storage buildings takes you on a journey through nearly a century of aeronautica, where in the dusty gloom of a warehouse, some of the world's most unique and famous aircraft await their return to the limelight. All of these aircraft or aviation artifacts are historically vital, either because of their unique record of accomplishment, or by their role in the general development of aerospace technology.

In a public display area of the Garber Facility stands one such example of the collection's historically significant aircraft: the Focke-Wulf 190. Looking as if it had just left the Bremen assembly works, its immaculate exterior belies its ability to take flight. The work being performed by the Garber Facility staff is not intended to meet the standards of airworthiness: though the Focke-Wulf 190 looks new and poised for battle, its fifty-year-old systems are likely too fragile to withstand the rigors of flight. The mission of NASM's Garber staff is not to *restore* the aircraft, but to *preserve* its original technology. In so doing, each of the aircraft's components are carefully cleaned and treated for long-term safekeeping and prepared as an exhibit in the scheme of aviation technology. The aircraft is essentially "pickled," retaining most of its original equipment. Future generations will find these artifacts much as they were originally built.

The job of preserving an airplane takes years of intense, and often tedious, labor. For this reason, the curatorial staff carefully plans and develops each project, in accordance with the future display requirements of the museum. One of the current projects on the shop floor is the Boeing B-29, *Enola Gay*, the world's first atomic bomber. It is planned for completion in 1995 for the fiftieth anniversary of its

Cockpit of NASM's Focke-Wulf 190F-8 shows the degree of detail in the preservation work being carried out at the Garber Facilty.

mission. Another project, the Aichi Seiran, is also a priority, but for a different reason: the Japanese submarine-based attack bomber was found to be rapidly deteriorating. Work has commenced to prevent its loss. For the same reason, the Hawker Hurricane IIC project is also underway. The staff at NASM works to preserve aviation's history, ensuring that these monuments of technological history will survive into the next century and beyond.

RECONSTRUCTING THE PAST: THE KINGFISHER

The word *historian* conjures up the image of a myopic scholar, sitting hunched over piles of books in dusty archives, endlessly leafing through volumes of antiquated documents. Generally, we wouldn't christen an airplane specialist with the title, *historian*. Yet, if we consider for a moment the impetus of the project, this may be a fitting description. Both the historian and the classic airplane specialist share an enduring commitment to reconstructing the past, and often both must undergo meticulous research, relentless tedium and unforgiving circumstances to realize the completion of their project.

For the historian the end product of his endeavor is the publication of a monograph; for the staff at the Garber facility, the end result is an aircraft, one of the best of the past.

In the corner of Building Twenty, in one of the facility's public display areas, stands one of the Navy's most uncelebrated workhorses: the Vought OS2U Kingfisher. Launched from a catapult system aboard a battleship, the little 450 horsepower floatplane was employed as an observation scout aircraft, which could land in the sea and be retrieved back aboard the ship by means of a crane. This type plane is credited with the rescue of famed World War I ace Eddie Rickenbacker and his crew, when their B-17 was ditched in the South Pacific. Unable to take off with the entire crew aboard, the pilot water-taxied his plane across forty miles of rough seas to safety.

As I was recalling this story, acting shop foreman, Bill Reese, pointed to the Kingfisher with a smile and said, somewhat dryly, "I have seven years of my life wrapped up in that airplane." Reese wasn't alone in his personal investment in this historic aircraft; a typical project takes seven years to complete, and the Garber technicians here have a dedication only surpassed perhaps by the builders of the ancient cathedrals.

After seven years of arduous, often tedious labor, very few people, I guessed, would be able to witness this piece of magnificent work. Reese seemed happy to find some gratitude in my interest in the plane. "The first four-and-a-half years," Reese continued, "were spent taking the airplane apart and preserving or restoring each individual component." He didn't seem bothered, however, by the lack of attention bestowed on his handiwork. I noted the satisfaction in his slight smile as he looked at the Kingfisher.

Reese explained that the aircraft had been on outdoor display by the Navy in Massachusetts and had been protected from the elements by heavy coatings of latex paint on the outside and additional coatings of zinc chromate on the inside. The main float and wing-tip floats didn't accompany the aircraft, but were secured at a later point in the project. The interior surfaces were cleaned free of the zinc chromate coatings with a walnut shell blaster and treated for corrosion. All of the Plexiglas was unusable, requiring the fabrication of wooden molds to make each of the curved panes. "A full set of tech orders was the saving grace in this project," adds Reese. He explained that many projects are undertaken without the benefit of any technical documentation. This can effectively double the time required to complete the project.

The documentation had specified every aspect of the Kingfisher's construction, including structure, mechanical linkages and electrical wiring. It even included information for paint and insignia marking dimensions. "Four-and-a-half years, Reese repeated, "of individual nuts, bolts, castings, extrusions, each cleaned and recoated." As he described the process, Reese's expression revealed the tedium of the project.

No work can be completed until you have all of the required materials, and sometimes this requires keen detective work. For the Kingfisher, the wing-tip floats were a special problem that required some NASM ingenuity.

I talked with Robert Mikesh, curator of aircraft for NASM during the Kingfisher project, who remembered well the process of acquiring the main and wing-tip floats: "We received the aircraft with conventional landing gear, but I felt it would be best represented in its float configuration." To locate a Kingfisher float, Mikesh placed an advertisement in *Trade-a-Plane* but, lacking response, began to look for other options. He contacted the float's original manufacturer, Edo-Aire, about constructing a new float. Fortunately, Edo succeeded in recovering a float from a crash site in Alaska, along with bracing wires and struts for the wing-tip floats. The float, however, was damaged and severed into three pieces and would require a lot of attention. "About this time," Mikesh continued with alacrity, "I received a call about a complete, but sort of crumpled float, buried under a pile of cars in a junk yard in Kodiak, Alaska." As luck would have it, a third float turned up in St. Petersburg, Florida, which was undamaged and complete. Edo-Aire sponsored the purchase of this float,

Vought OS2U Kingfisher.

Cockpit of NASM's Kingfisher scout plane.

and soon afterward, it was delivered to Andrews AFB, a few miles from the Garber facility. Mikesh said that the wing-tip floats were found in New Smyrna Beach, Florida, owned by an aircraft parts dealer, where they had been lashed together to make a small fishing craft. The Kingfisher project could then continue. The parts from Alaska and the wing-tip floats from Florida provided sufficient materials to complete the aircraft.

In addition to the problematic task of obtaining parts, there is the formidable project of reconstructing the aircraft. The Kingfisher's control system was unique for its day, employing both ailerons and spoilers on the wing surface for roll control. Reese demonstrated the lowering of the flaps, by hand-crank, which also angled the ailerons down to effect a full span flap for improved takeoffs and landing on the sea. "All of the linkages are rigged within the cockpit area," he explained, "with a complex series of bellcranks, gearing and chains, which interlink the control stick, the flap crank, and each of the respective surfaces." The rigging was a frustrating job, getting all of the cable tensions and control surfaces to work in concert. An inadvertent reversal of one of the attachments defied Reese and partner, Bob Padgett, for several days, while they unraveled the problem. As Reese described to me the challenges of final assembly of the Kingfisher, he remarked once again on the time involved in the project: "Roughly in the last year-and-a-half of work, when the pieces are assembled into sub-assemblies and the sub-assemblies into a fuselage, you finally begin to feel some accomplishment for the first four-and-a-half years of labor."

After my orientation to the Kingfisher, Reese allowed me to occupy the cockpit. Sitting in the pilot's seat, the detail was evident. Everything was immaculate: the operating placards, instrument markings, map case, complete with pencil holders, and the folding map table were each present according to specification. These accessories attested to the nature of the long-range scout mission for which the Kingfisher was intended. The breech of the fixed, forward firing, 30-caliber Colt Browning machine gun, with its ammunition feed and storage mechanism, were conveniently placed beneath the panel and between the pilot's legs for functional access. The windscreen was punctuated by a magnifying aiming sight, which was indicative of the anti-submarine and shipping attack roles in which the airplane was employed.

I then was invited to climb into the aft crew station, which required some agility, the seat being contained within a gimbal-mounted machine gun turret. The second crewman was a radio operator, gunner and copilot, with a complete set of flight controls. Releasing the gimbal lock in the turret allowed the entire seat and gun ring to rotate together, allowing full traverse of the 30-caliber gun. While aiming the gun to the vertical position, the seat rotated back to a fully reclined position, requiring very little physical effort. Facing forward, the radio operator's view was restricted by an ADF homing receiver and loop antenna. It appeared that the copilot's flying duties were limited to relief pilot on longer duration patrols and landings, in the event the pilot was injured or killed.

It was too easy to admire the completed aircraft and romanticize about working in this historic environment, without considering the degree of intensive labor and tedium involved. There's not much recognition that comes from the Garber staff's personal investment of time and labor. People like Bill Reese are compensated instead by a kind a personal satisfaction in having a hand in preserving our technological heritage.

THE GARBER STAFF

As I observed the various other projects, each occurring simultaneously, and learned more of what each project entailed, I quickly discovered that the logistics involved in coordinating one of the projects were overwhelming. The disassembly and careful cataloging of parts, the construction of new parts, often without any kind of documentation, the removal of wings, tail surfaces, engines, system linkages, fluid lines, wiring, and all associated mechanical, hydraulic and electric actuators — the amount of work and time required for one project alone seemed insurmountable. To give you an example, I observed for some minutes Will Lee, who was busy at work on the cockpit of a Hurricane, among its myriad instrumentation and controls. I learned that each item had to be removed, cleaned and repaired and then, if necessary, treated for corrosion. Different materials required different kinds of attention. For example, metals often went to the chemical specialist to undergo the processes of etching and conversion coating to render them preserved. Other parts would simply be cleaned and painted with an appropriate clear acrylic or lacquer. Mechanical linkages and assemblies were lubricated with a synthetic red grease, then reassembled. Electric motors had to be disassembled for cleaning and repaired as necessary, but not rewound or tested, so as to preserve their original windings.

Spending just a few hours at the Garber facility was enough to realize that the reconstruction of a fifty-year-old airplane entails much more than I had ever imagined. And, as Mikesh's story illustrates, finding parts sometimes involves keen detective work, often taking months, even years, to discover and procure. When parts can't be found, NASM must depend on their in-house specialists to research and fabricate them from raw materials. The facility employs thirteen technicians, including four specialists: one welder/fabricator, one machinist and two chemists. The remaining nine technicians are assigned to a particular project and, when needed, will draw on the expertise of the specialists.

Another member of the staff, Bernie Poppert, was busy at work on the B-29's ailerons, elevators and rudder control surfaces, recovering them with original specification linens, dopes, and rib stitching techniques. Nearby, engine specialist George Genotti was proceeding with the overhaul of one of the B-29's Wright 3350 engines. During reassembly, he explained to me that the familiar red synthetic grease would replace the normal engine oil. In addition to providing necessary lubrication of the pistons and bearings, the red grease also helps to preserve the engine's internal components for the long term. Although the engine will never be run, Genotti precisely set the functional adjustments of the valves, carburetor and timing according to operational specifications.

Where does one find a specialist in preserving World War II aircraft? I asked myself this question as I walked through a warehouse at the Garber facility and saw others, like Poppert, Genotti and Lee, amid complex arrays of dismembered and disassembled aircraft. They worked with a persistent deliberation, characterizing a scientist on the verge of a new breakthrough. Certainly the technology of this golden age of aviation requires a different kind of know-how than those trained to work on contemporary jets. When I asked the different staff members what kind of expertise had qualified them for the job, I found their backgrounds so varied that it was impossible to make a tenable generalization. Anne McCoombs, who was working on the wing and engine sections of the B-29, had an aeronautical engineering degree and an airframe and powerplant mechanic's license; Matt Nazzarro, who was working in the cockpit of a Seiran, had forfeited his occupation as a glassblower to come to the Garber facility; and Will Lee had been employed by a prosthetics manufacturer. Although each staff member comes to the facility with a different background, there's a common thread among all of these people: a keen interest in airplanes and aviation history.

When these specialists have finished most of their work and the airplane is structurally complete, it's ready for the final touches. This isn't as easy as selecting the colors of paint and markings that suit the personal taste of the detailer. Instead, it requires careful research to determine not only the proper hues, but also the specific types of paint to be used. The curators carefully choose each particular color and marking to accord with the historical nature of the aircraft. Most aircraft are finished

Bernie Poppert stitches linen onto *Enola Gay's* elevator control surface.

George Genotti overhauling one of the
Wright 3350 engines for the Enola Gay.

Between the Seiran's float and fuselage, volunteer Derek Hodge
(foreground) and staff member Matt Nazzarro contemplate
the repair of a wooden cockpit fixture.

in the same colors and markings as they had when they arrived at the facility. Upon completion of the five- to seven-year project, one might mistakenly assume it ready for transport to the museum in Washington, D.C. Not quite. Again, because of space limitations, most aircraft are stored in a Garber facility warehouse, where they await the call for exhibition.

WARRIORS IN CAPTIVITY

In Building Seven rests the most significant segment of NASM's collection of captured Japanese and German warplanes. In a dimly lit space, a silent pall surrounds the ghostly shapes of the enemy warplanes in captivity. Looming in the shadows, their sleek silhouettes are devoid of color and visible detail. These one-of-a-kind aircraft, stored in cramped rows and dismembered of their wings, as if to ensure their captivity, are the sole surviving examples of their kind. The Luftwaffe's Heinkel He 219 night fighter, the Messerschmitt Me 410 twin-engine bomber-destroyer, the Blohm und Voss Bv 155 experimental high altitude interceptor, and the Junkers Ju 388L high altitude reconnaissance bomber — each aircraft quietly awaits its fate in the subdued light. These specialized night and high altitude aircraft are examples of late war developments, which reflect the defensive posture Germany had been forced to assume under around-the-clock bombardment.

Alongside these examples of German ingenuity are members of Japan's late war technology: the unique Kyushu J7W1 Shinden (Magnificent Lightning), a sleek canard pusher engine fighter; the Kawanishi N1K1 Kyofu (Mighty Wind) floatplane fighter; and the Yokosuka P1Y1-C Ginga (Milky Way) bomber. Additionally, a rare turbojet powered trainer version of the Yokosuka MXY-7 Ohka 11 suicide bomber, and the Nakajima Ki-115 Tsurugi, a crude sheet steel construction, radial engine suicide plane, survive as examples of Japan's desperation to turn the tide of the conflict.

These vintage German and Japanese aircraft are not without their famous and unique American counterparts. The jet black Northrop P-61C Black Widow, twin-engine night fighter, and the two-hundred-mission veteran, Martin B-26 Marauder, *Flak Bait*, await their return to the public eye. Also in storage, the experimental Curtiss XP-55 Ascender, canard design, and the Northrop XP-56 tailless interceptor, survive as examples of extremes in American fighter development. These are but a few of the rare survivors of the Second World War, which await the curator's call.

Additional Rare Survivors
In Garber Storage

JAPANESE AIRCRAFT

Nakajima J1N1 Gekko (IRVING)
twin-engine night fighter

Nakajima B6N2 Tenzan (JILL)
shipboard torpedo bomber

Aichi B7A1 Ryusei (GRACE)
shipboard attack bomber

Nakajima C6N1 Saiun (MYRT)
reconnaissance bomber

Nakajima Kikka (Experimental)
twinjet fighter-bomber

Kawanishi N1K1 Shiden (GEORGE)
single-engine fighter

GERMAN AIRCRAFT

Focke-Wulf 190F-8 Wurger
single-engine fighter-bomber

Dornier Do 335 Pfeil
twin-engine interceptor

Messerschmitt Me 163 Komet
rocket powered interceptor

Arado Ar.234B Blitz
twinjet bomber

Gotha Go.229 (Experimental)
twinjet all wing fighter

Heinkel He 162 "Volksjäger"
single-engine jet fighter

Although dozens of rare aircraft seem to cry out for refurbishment, curatorial demands must take priority. At the time of my visit to the Garber facility, three particular aircraft had this priority: the Hawker Hurricane, the Seiran, and the *Enola Gay*.

THE HURRICANE

In Building Ten, the skeletal frame of the Hawker Hurricane fuselage awaited the completion of its wood former and stringer sections, which were being fabricated in England. The Rolls-Royce Merlin was ready for mating to the engine mount structure, while finishing touches were being applied to the cockpit instrumentation.

The Hurricane represents a major technological transition in the design of the British fighter. Built in quantity during the late 1930s, the Hurricane bridged the gap between the wood and fabric fixed-gear biplane, and the modern all-metal, low-wing, retractable gear monoplanes of the next generation. The British fighter is testimony to this changeover: it retains some of the fabric-covered wood structure in the fuselage and was originally fitted with a fixed-pitch wooden propeller. Available in service in the autumn of 1940, the Hurricane held the line while the Spitfire was being rushed to RAF squadrons to meet the onslaught of the Luftwaffe.

Will Lee used a Geiger counter to determine which of the cockpit instruments could be safely dismantled. Radium or tritium were commonly utilized to provide luminescence for aircraft instruments during the period, and they presented an exposure hazard. Several of the Hurricane's instruments were highly active on the Geiger counter and had to be left in their existing condition. Since the original Hawker parts catalog was scantily illustrated, Lee had to rely on documentation made during disassembly, as he carefully replaced the cockpit instrumentation. Because of the complexity of such a project, the reassembly of components sometimes occurs years after disassembly. Lee further explained, with some modesty, that even after years of work with the airplane, the job is still thoroughly challenging: "Though the electrical schematics are fairly straightforward, the parts listing and designations are difficult to understand, at best." Perched on his bench stool, examining some minuscule instrument screws, his comments enhanced my impression of the dedication each of these people bring to their work.

The Hawker Hurricane IIC's instrument panel nearing completion.

The complex tubular steel structure of the Hurricane awaits the wooden formers and stringers which will give the fuselage its final shape.

This particular airframe is actually a combination of parts from several Hurricanes, acquired in a trade with the RAF. It will be finished to represent a typical fighter variant, since there is no history specific to this aircraft.

THE SEIRAN

Matt Nazzaro's project was the Aichi M6A1 Seiran (Mountain Haze). At the end of the war, this particular Seiran was captured intact in Japan and then transported to the United States for evaluation. The aircraft was acquired by NASM, through General Arnold's initiative, to preserve examples of Japanese and German combat aircraft. This unique aircraft was designed to fulfill a proposal by the Japanese Navy to build a 4,500-ton displacement submarine, with a cruising radius of over forty-one thousand nautical miles. The submarine was to house two Seiran aircraft in watertight cylindrical hangars, for catapult launch against targets well outside the normal range of Japanese naval aircraft. The primary target envisaged was the Panama Canal. Though the I-400 class submarine was completed by the termination of hostilities, the Panama Canal mission was not carried out.

Although it came to the Garber facility largely intact, the airplane had spent a long period in outside storage and suffered considerable damage. Unfortunately, virtually no documentation was available for the aircraft, and so during disassembly, the Garber staff had to expend a considerable effort determining exactly what each system was, and systematically cataloging each part. This was no easy project as some of these systems were fairly complex. The wings, for example, were designed to fold along the rear spar, to lie flat along the sides of the fuselage while stored in the submarine hangar. The vertical fin folds at the top and the horizontal stabilizer also folds down at the tips. The Seiran's liquid-cooled inverted V-12 engine stands vertically mounted next to the airplane and appears almost new. It is estimated the aircraft may have had only a few hours of flight test completed before its capture.

The cockpit instrumentation was spread out on a table in the work area, with most of the cleaning and preservation work completed and awaiting reinstallation. Some of the instruments were unfamiliar to the technicians, and in order to discover their function, the Garber staff had to enlist interpreters to determine the meaning of the markings on the instruments. The preservation of the marking detail in the cockpit is witness to the meticulous attention devoted to avoiding alterations or improvements on the original aircraft.

Fully preserved attitude instrument ready for installation in the Seiran floatplane.

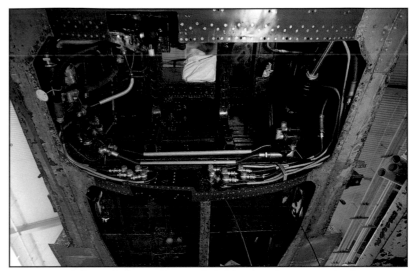

Viewed from below, some of the hydraulic controls for the Seiran's folding wing mechanism.

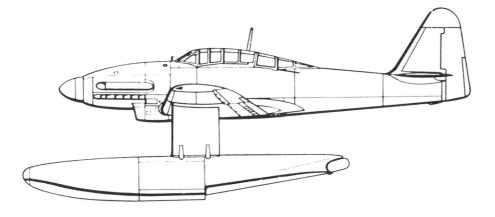

The Seiran is mounted to a mobile work stand as work progresses inside the cockpit area.

Japanese interpreters have assisted in determining what each instrument measures.

Nazzarro and partner Robert McLean have spent a good deal of effort in the cockpit area, cleaning and treating corroded areas, while preserving as much of the original coatings and metal as possible. A wood floor section in the rear cockpit had suffered sufficient degradation to require its replacement with all new wood construction. A layout of the rotted parts provided enough evidence, combined with the known position of the flooring, to construct a new section with the aid of some conjecture.

Technicians Nazzarro and McLean have developed such a keen eye for detail that they can read this plane's technology like a history book. For example, Nazzarro pointed to evidence that the development of this aircraft was a rushed, even hasty process: a hole had been made in a piece of structure by means of "gang drilling" a circular series of small holes. What was particularly odd about this was that the hole was never used for any purpose. Furthermore, the formed aluminum parts removed from the aircraft exhibited a type of brittleness attributed to "work hardening" of the metal. This implied that the aluminum had been hammered to shape by unskilled laborers, rather than mechanically pressed by conventional machinery. Although the technology preserved herein is somewhat crude, it exemplifies the stress under which the Japanese aircraft industry was forced to operate, under nightly B-29 raids.

THE ENOLA GAY

Perhaps the largest, most ambitious project undertaken by National Air and Space Museum is the Boeing B-29 Superfortress, the *Enola Gay*. The fuselage components have been largely completed, and the wings, engines and tail group were being prepared for final assembly. Senior advisor, Donald Lopez, described a plan by the director to bring the completed bomber into Washington and build a temporary display structure over it on the mall, adjacent to the museum, for the fiftieth anniversary of the bomber's 1945 Hiroshima mission. Aside from any public relations considerations, the plan was determined to be too costly to carry out. A planned display and preservation facility at the Dulles Airport, large enough to store all of the aircraft housed at the Garber facility and to display the B-29 and other large aircraft, was anticipated when the *Enola Gay* project was commenced. That plan, however, is on indefinite hold, due to current economic conditions; it is likely that only the bomber's nose section will be placed on display in the museum in 1995.

Bernie Poppert, who has worked on the B-29 since the project began in 1984, gave me the tour through the inside of the giant Superfortress. In its multi-paned

The Confederate Air Force's "Fifi" is the only Boeing B-29 flying today.

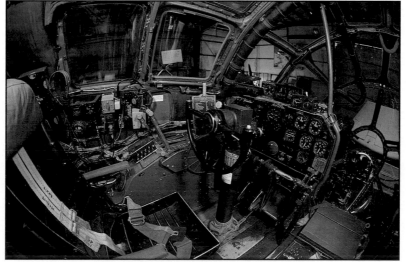

Pilot's position of B-29 *Enola Gay*.

Glazed nose enclosure of *Enola Gay's* cockpit stations.

nose enclosure, the bombardier, pilot, copilot and engineer stations were all within a few feet of each other. The walk-in cockpit featured two separate instrument panels with separate sets of power controls for the pilot and copilot. The bombardier accessed his compartment by moving between the two pilot stations and stepping down into the nose of the bomber. The flight engineer faced aft, opposite the bulkhead behind the copilot's station, with a complete set of instrumentation for all of the aircraft's electrical, hydraulic and pneumatic systems.

Poppert stressed that the majority of work on the *Enola Gay* involved cleaning off dirt, grease and debris and applying protective coatings. Only in localized areas did external factors cause corrosion or deterioration. The degree of wear on the floors and consoles indicated the relatively low total time accumulated on the aircraft before it was acquired by NASM. The bomber made several crossings of the Pacific after the war, in anticipation of further nuclear testing, but it was eventually retired to the custody of NASM in 1949. During its brief postwar career, a number of modifications were made to the aircraft, which changed some of the original equipment. One of the challenges of the project was to restore all of the original furnishings of its August 6, 1945, mission.

The nose section was moved into Building Ten in December 1984, when Rich Horigan and Dave Peterson began work in the cockpit. The nose section extends aft to include the dual bomb bays, more than one-half of the bomber's ninety-nine foot length. Karl Heinzel joined the project when work on the bomb bays began. Extensive cleaning was performed in this section, which was specially modified to carry the nuclear device. The bomb rack designed to carry the "Little Boy" had been removed from the aircraft by the Air Force when it was acquired by NASM. The drawings had to be specially declassified for reproduction of the bomb rack by the Garber team. Overhead in the bomb bay, a tube joins the cockpit area to the tail section, allowing access from one section to the other, while the compartments are pressurized.

In 1988, the tail section was moved into the shop area, where work began in the tail-gunner's compartment. It was here that the most serious damage had been sustained from weathering. "Apparently the aft hatch had fallen in and smashed the wooden flooring," Poppert recalls, "and of course then the weather, the birds and mice got in," causing the deterioration of the interior fabric liner and the canvas boot fairing around the guns. From the Garber facility archives, the engineering drawings provided the patterns and fabric specifications to duplicate the rotted material and effect its replacement. The tail guns on the *Enola Gay* were the only defensive armament on the aircraft, as operated by the 509th composite wing. A pair of

Bombardier's control panel in extreme nose of *Enola Gay*.

The single defensive station of the *Enola Gay*, the tail-gunner's compartment.

50-caliber machine guns were obtained and the computer-aided gunsight over-hauled to complete the two-year restoration of this compartment. To exit the tail turret, the gunner crawls forward through a pressure bulkhead, then through a narrow space between the ammunition boxes and feed mechanisms for his guns, over the tail skid housing, along a narrow passage between a series of oxygen bottles, to the radar operator's compartment.

Poppert explained that at some point in 1947, the original APQ-13 radar was upgraded to an APQ-23 unit. The radar was used to accurately designate the target, even in inclement weather. A small black "bulb" protruded from the belly, between the two bomb bays, containing the radar dish. In returning the radar operator's station to its original configuration, a number of items had to be located, which has required some creative thinking. The arrangement of the radar station varied from group to group and, in the case of the 509th, information was available to duplicate the table and instrumentation as it was originally installed in this airplane. A few items still remain to be located, including the radar's azimuth control box.

Under routine service procedure, the flight controls were scheduled for recovering periodically, whether needed or not. In this fashion, the maintenance crew simply removed the rudder, elevators, and ailerons and exchanged them with a recovered set. Accordingly, the flight controls on the *Enola Gay* were determined to be substantially older than the rest of the airplane. The present covering is one hundred percent cotton, per specification, but the dope treatment was a little heavier than specification. Following stitching of the fabric to the control surface, the cotton was treated with a fungicidal dope. Next, four coats of nitrate dope were applied. Nitrate dope cures to a certain point, then stops shrinking. Several coats of aluminum pigmented clear butyrate dope were then applied over the nitrate, to provide reflective protection of the cotton from ultraviolet light. A final coating of butyrate completed the process. Although the butyrate dope continues to shrink with time, it can effectively "slide" over the nitrate layer, and it is substantially less flammable than the nitrate dope. The Air Force had a system of documenting the coatings applied, and the date of application on the control surface itself. Poppert pointed out the markings applied by NASM which showed both the date and the order in which the coatings were applied to the surface.

The restoration of the inboard wing sections was the project of Karl Heinzel, Anne McCoombs and Bob Padgett. McCoombs described a minor setback in the project: "My partner was examining an area in the number three engine nacelle and found a large bird's nest between the firewall and the wing spar." The birds had left quite an accumulation of droppings which had caused considerable corrosion. The discovery necessitated removal of the nacelle from the wing. Bob Padgett was delicately removing surface corrosion within the nacelle using a green plastic abrasive pad on a small orbital sander. The turbo-superchargers have been overhauled and coated with clear acrylic preservative. Electric cowl flap actuators have been disassembled, cleaned and repaired as necessary, and similarly coated. Two of the Wright 3350-57 Cyclone engines had been completed in Building Ten by George Genotti. The remaining two engines were being overhauled by the San Diego Aerospace Museum, under an NASM supervised program.

Since a display site for the *Enola Gay* has not been officially determined, it is not known whether the plane will be fully assembled upon completion. The *Enola Gay*, and other very large aircraft in the collection, may have to wait for the anticipated Dulles facility before being completely assembled for display.

"CORROSION WARFARE"

Behind the scenes, almost hidden in the back recesses of Garber Facility's Building Ten, is a section marked *Corrosion Warfare Unit*. It is here that the most specialized and detailed part of the preservation process is accomplished. Two rows of submersion tanks create a chemical "gauntlet" through which weathered and corroded parts are subjected to treatments ranging from cleaning to electroplating. Components removed from the aircraft vary in material from steel, aluminum, brass and copper, to wood, rubber and plastics. NASM's conservator is responsible for the ongoing research to determine the best methods of corrosion control and inhibition, cleaning techniques, and protective coatings available. Specialist Bayne Rector has worked in the chemical section for fifteen years and performs the delicate electroplating processes, while supervising staff members in the use of more general treatments.

THE ENEMY

To explain the preservation methods, specifically for metals, Rector refreshed some of my basic college chemistry. Corrosion, commonly known as rust, is the life struggle of all metals. Rust is the product of a chemical reaction between the metal and atmospheric oxygen. Moisture, also present in the atmosphere, serves to accelerate the process of corrosion by penetrating the rust layer and providing oxygen, in the form of water, to react with the metal.

Hawker Hurricane wing before corrosion control....

... and after.

In addition to these external factors, metals, because of their molecular makeup, have a certain self-destructing tendency. Metallic surfaces are composed of microscopic "ridges" of positive and negative electrical charges, which also react with each other, causing the metal to slowly deteriorate.

A third, and more destructive type of degradation, is intergranular corrosion, or exfoliation, which starts within the metal itself. Exfoliation results from a contamination of the liquid alloy during casting, or from a slow separating of elements in the alloy over time, causing flaking or peeling. It is most common in cast or extruded structural members, and in most cases, parts with extensive intergranular corrosion must be replaced.

PREPARATION FOR BATTLE

Any airplane which has spent a great deal of time sitting outdoors has suffered some degree of corrosive damage. This damage is compounded with layers of grease, dirt and carbon which build up during normal operation. During the first phase of preservation, parts are thoroughly cleaned to remove contaminants and reveal the extent of corrosion. Depending on the number of factors — the type of material, the amount of buildup and the extent of corrosive damage — the cleaning process may involve only a mild soap solution, or the use of a stronger sodium hydroxide treatment. Sometimes these treatments aren't enough, and to remove paint and corrosion, a part may require bead blasting or vigorous scrubbing. Instrument casings and delicate parts may need to be treated in solutions with ultrasonic agitation. This treatment helps to reach into recesses and cavities which are not accessible using normal abrasive methods. Regardless of which treatment is applied to materials in this first stage of the preservation process, it is extremely important to remove any chemical or abrasive residue left from this cleaning phase. If this residue were not removed, it could promote further damage and corrosion to the material.

A STRONG DEFENSE

Once corrosion has been effectively removed, the metal surface is treated with a mild acid wash to ensure the adherence of the coatings. To protect against surface corrosion, coatings are generally accepted as the best defense. Historically, zinc chromate has been used extensively for primer coatings since it tends to neutralize the charge distribution of the metal's surface. Additional paint coatings limit the exposure to atmospheric oxygen and moisture to further inhibit corrosion.

Steel forgings removed from the wings of the *Enola Gay* were designed as tracks on which the wing flaps traversed during extension. Boeing selected a cadmium plating process to protect the steel surface from corrosion and provide a durable surface to roll the heavy flap bearings over. In this fashion, a bright silver cadmium layer is subjected to the effects of oxidation, rather than the structural steel of the flap track. Rector demonstrated the electro-chemical plating process and the newly plated flap tracks, ready for reinstallation.

To maintain the integrity of the plane's original makeup, all of the various coating processes were available to Garber specialists, and surfaces were recoated with the same material used in original manufacture. Where no coatings were used originally, a clear acrylic is applied to protect the metal. The use of wax is also gaining favor as a surface coating, since it is reversible. The original insignia markings on the *Enola Gay* will most likely be coated with a microcrystalline wax, for their preservation, and then painted over to display them as they originally appeared.

PRESERVING OTHER MATERIALS

Shop foreman Rich Horigan had taken a temporary leave from his office to perform a special project on the tail section of the Focke-Wulf Ta 152H. I wanted to see how the preservation process differed for wood and other materials used in aircraft construction.

This rare and unique Luftwaffe fighter was a special high altitude variant of the Fw 190 series fighters and, interestingly, displays some of the material problems encountered by the German aircraft industry in 1944-45. Wood was commonly used in many aircraft, in small structures and detail components. Flooring, containers and other utility items in various aircraft were constructed of plywood or spruce, because they were lightweight and relatively easy to construct. In the Focke-Wulf, the entire empennage and extreme aft fuselage were constructed of wood, while most of the rest of the aircraft retained the traditional aluminum structures. The aircraft utilized a sealed pressure cabin, which featured an instrument panel also made of wood. The plane's horizontal stabilizer and elevators had become badly deteriorated, requiring immediate attention. Exposed to the effects of moisture, the plywood had delaminated. Horrigan had discovered the cause of this damage, noting for me a furry mess of what had once been home to some mice. As usual, all original items

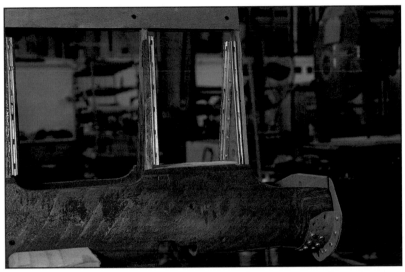

Preserved elevator control structure of Focke-Wulf Ta 152H.

Deteriorated wood of opposite elevator.

Markings depict repaired and duplicate replacement parts of the Ta 152H.

The Ta 15H's horizontal stablizer incorporated a unique paper composite leading edge.

were being retained wherever possible, but some sections needed to be replaced with new wood. These pieces had been stamped appropriately with the marking, "repaired by NASM" or "NASM duplicate," with the date. The stabilizer's leading edge was formed of a laminate of paper and glue, which made a very hard, yet lightweight, composite material. Horigan's expertise with woodworking was evident in the finished sections. His expertise would also be employed to complete the wood structure of the Hawker Hurricane fuselage. The remainder of the Ta 152H was not scheduled for preservation and remained in storage in Building Seven.

Other types of materials required special handling to reverse the effects of weathering and deterioration. Almost all of the World War II airplanes have Plexiglas canopies or windows which, when left to prolonged exposure, become "crazed" or yellowed. Where possible, these have been returned to their original clarity by careful buffing of the plastic. In an extremely time-consuming procedure, electrical wire bundles have been removed, unbundled, and each individual wire cleaned and tested prior to rebundling and replacement in the airplane. Rubber weatherstripping and seals have been rejuvenated with lubricants, where possible, to avoid replacement.

The tide is being slowly turned in the war against corrosion. The level of technical expertise being applied in Building Ten, promises to provide a strong defense against the effects of time and the elements. Each airplane emerging from the Garber facility will likely survive for a few more generations, leaving a clear record of the past.

SPECIALTY DEPARTMENTS

THE GARBER POWERPLANT COLLECTION

Building Eleven at the Garber facility houses a collection of unique and rare aero-engines, ranging from the earliest reciprocating types to exotic, experimental turbine and rocket powerplants. The powerplant collection hosts a substantial variety of one-of-a-kind examples of 1940s technological developments. The evolutionary period of aviation saw the reciprocating internal combustion engine reach its zenith, while also witnessing the successful development and application of the gas turbine. Rows of German-made Heinkel, BMW, and Junkers turbojets share storage with some of the most exotic reciprocating aircraft engines ever built. The British Napier Sabre IIA 24-cylinder, 2180 hp, liquid-cooled horizontal "H" configured engine of the Hawker Typhoon, and the Chrysler XIV-2220, a 16-cylinder, 2300 hp, liquid-cooled inverted-vee engine of the Republic XP-47H Thunderbolt exemplify the little-known extent of development in powerplant technology during the early 1940s.

THE GARBER ARCHIVES

Next to the shop facilities, in Building Twelve, an air-conditioned, humidity controlled storage unit houses the Garber Facility Archives. Contained here, and of use to the specialist or researcher, are copies of the original manufacturers' and U.S. government's documentation for many of the aircraft. Parts catalogs, operating handbooks, service and maintenance manuals, and other technical orders are available for most U.S. built aircraft. Also available are microfilm copies of the original engineering drawings. The archives have a separate staff managing the storage, maintenance and use of the aircraft documents. Due to staff and space limitations, research in this facility is by appointment only.

During my first two visits here, I was met by NASM archivist, Larry Wilson. After I explained the nature of my project and my intention to reproduce some of the microfilms and technical orders, he handed me a pair of white cotton gloves for handling the collection's documents and then familiarized me with the microfilm reader. Wilson impressed me in much the same way the technicians had in Building Ten — he was knowledgeable in his field of expertise, but more importantly, he showed a genuine interest in airplanes and their history. His job was to locate, out of thousands of files of documents, the specific documents I requested. While working with me, he noted the status of the document, as part of an ongoing effort to upgrade the condition of the collection. The U.S. Air Force supplied most of the material in varying states of disorder, creating a huge job for the staff. At the time I visited, the archivists were organizing the files, compiling complete versions of each document from incomplete copies, and upgrading them with the latest revisions.

Paul Garber's work in establishing the National Air and Space Museum collection and providing for the safe storage of its aircraft and artifacts have created an invaluable national asset. The future of this vast treasure demands the continued level of expertise practiced by the Garber staff, and hopefully, the accommodation of greatly increased display space.

Chuck Yeager's "Glamourous Glen III" P-51D Mustang

CHAPTER 4

The Photoflight

For nearly ten years, the image of the scarlet red Warhawk, first seen on the cover of an aviation magazine when I was a boy, had captured my imagination, etched itself into my memory and lingered in my subconscious. I had already been fascinated with the airplane, but, I suppose seeing the photograph stirred some kind of artistic inclination inside me as well. I soon began to investigate the workings of my father's range finder, with rather well-defined intentions of combining my interest in both airplanes and photography.

I experimented with an assortment of cameras and darkroom equipment and then set out to find some subjects with which to work. The local airport worked pretty well, offering me plenty of activity, as I stood near the approach end of the runway trying to get close to some airplanes in flight. Parked nearby, a pair of derelict B-25 firebombers caught my attention; these were, in fact, real World War II Mitchells, but unfortunately they were also very still and lifeless. These birds really deserved to be rendered in their natural element.

After a brief detour through college and then establishing a means of making a living, the scarlet red Warhawk came back to haunt me again, like the beckoning sirens that tempted Odysseus. In response to this call, I tried to persuade the owners of nearly four hundred of the fighters and bombers to allow me to attempt the elusive in-flight portraiture. I'm not exactly sure what I had expected, but the next four years took me on a whirlwind tour of the country, meeting and working with some fascinating people and consuming copious quantities of Kodachrome film.

My first trip took me to meet Alan Henley, a cattleman, in Geiger, Alabama. I didn't know it at the time, but our association-turned-friendship would have a profound effect on the progress of my endeavor. Alan and I had quite a lot in common: we both had a genuine interest in the warplanes and seemed to work well together in the close formation photo work. In an unusually beautiful setting, we circled the lush green Alabama countryside, in unwavering formation, as the late daylight played on the silver and blue Mustang before my fascinated eyes.

Considering the fact that I had never been in a T-6 and had never seriously taken in-flight portraits, I felt very fortunate to get a few good photographs, and even more fortunate to be recommended to some of the other people in the area. The two of us were, shortly thereafter, invited to Troy, Alabama, as the guests of Wiley Sanders. It was there that I met Earl Smith and all of Wiley's airport employees who, through their interest and enthusiasm for my proposed project, have made it a realization.

The most effective place to shoot in-flight portraiture is from an airplane with an open tail position suitable for the purpose. As it turns out, no airplane of this type is widely available, and the few that are consume roughly 150 to 200 gallons of fuel per hour! Consequently, when the opportunity presented itself to shoot from the tail-gunner's position of Sanders' B-25, I came prepared. I was, quite honestly, pretty nervous about having some kind of equipment failure or judgement error interfere with this opportunity. Neither happened, thankfully, as we made about a half dozen flights over a period of three days. The resulting photographs were every bit what I had hoped for.

Wiley Sanders' B-25J "Ol Gray Mare."

Warbirds Air Museum's P-47D Thunderbolt.

I had, over the course of my first year, experienced about every mistake a person could make, including nearly getting myself pitched out of the back seat of an open T-6. But as I gained experience, spent more time planning, performed regular maintenance on the camera equipment, and accumulated a touch more common sense, I began to develop a little confidence in my ability to get the pictures I wanted.

A photographer *must* be able to communicate with his subject, and while in flight, this can present quite a challenge. Some people have been successful using hand signals, but I decided to try to shoot and talk to my subjects simultaneously, which required the use of a radio. So, I strapped a portable radio to my belt, installed a transmitter button on my camera's motor drive, and donned a canvas headset with a boom-mike, to solve the seemingly simple communications problem. Through all of the photoflights, the single greatest difficulty I encountered was keeping the myriad of wires and plugs connected and the correct buttons pushed. Several people can attest to these problems and my obsession with the radio gear!

I solved the problem of weightlessness in the open cockpit of the photo plane, by having a harness made — like a parachute with no chute — that strapped me to some portion of the aircraft's structure. In this fashion, I could work in an open cockpit, without the restraint of a seat belt. This piece of equipment never presented any serious problems.

Wiley Sanders' B-25, *Georgia Mae*, was specially adapted by mechanic-photographer Robert Smith to have the tail-gunner's position completely open for photo work. After his first attempt at riding in the open tail, Smith reported that the turbulent air in the opening made it nearly impossible to operate a camera there. With some further modifications, the situation was corrected shortly before I arrived.

I learned to adapt to the cramped space in the (still somewhat turbulent) tail opening and found various ways of utilizing the incredible perspective to advantage. Since the view is nearly unlimited — straight down, straight up . . . you name it — you can use it creatively to position your subject wherever you like. A very wide angle lens could take advantage of this unusual perspective, taking in all of the available background. The only trouble with the wide perspective was the fact that the subject needed to be within about ten feet of the tail of the B-25. I'm sure the two guys driving the B-25 didn't really want to know what was transpiring directly behind their airplane!

It was in this respect that I depended on Alan Henley's ability to put the airplane precisely where I wanted it, but no closer than he felt safe. Alan was entrusted by Wiley Sanders to fly all of the airplanes in the hangar, which we proceeded to photograph over the next eighteen months. We flew twice a day, once in the morning and then again in the late afternoon, often working until after dark. A long, narrow lake along the Georgia-Alabama border provided the backdrop I wanted, especially for the TBM Avenger which, being a Navy airplane, just looked better over water.

As we continued the process, Earl Smith, who was responsible for all of this serious business, decided that the subject pilots should wear khaki shirts and officer's caps while having their pictures taken. I took this theme one step further and purchased an original leather helmet, British two-paned flying goggles, Mae West floatation gear, and a couple of A-14 oxygen masks. When I showed up with a suitcase full of paraphernalia, the smart pilots turned and headed the other way, but there were always a few who had that Hollywood style.

On my last trip to Troy, instead of photographing some pilots dressed up like heroes, we photographed some rather distinguished pilots who didn't need to disguise themselves. The mission had been planned for some months by the Experimental Aircraft Association's Connie Bowlin, to bring some historic airplanes and

357th Fighter Group's Aces, left to right: "Tommy" Hayes, "Kit" Carson, "Chuck" Yeager, "Pete" Peterson and "Bud" Anderson.

pilots together for a sort of reunion. When I arrived at Troy, I was introduced to a very tall and familiar looking gentleman, David Hartman. In quick succession, I was thrusting my hand out to meet Clarence "Bud" Anderson and Charles "Chuck" Yeager. Both were distinguished P-51 Mustang pilots with the 357th fighter group, Eighth Air Force, in England during 1944 and 1945. Our flight of two B-25s and seven Mustangs proceeded to Oshkosh, Wisconsin, where we met with three other distinguished pilots of the 357th: Richard "Pete" Peterson, Leonard "Kit" Carson and Thomas "Tommy" Hayes. The five had been invited as the special guests of the EAA for their annual fly-in and convention and were to be recognized for their distinguished service.

In a special evening engagement at the EAA's *Theater in the Woods*, moderator David Hartman conducted a candid interview with five vibrant and eloquent Mustang aces. A respectful calm descended on an audience of over five thousand, as the first question was posed and these men began to reveal their experiences in the air war over Europe, fifty years prior. In the tradition of the best of storytellers, the firsthand accounts related events which intertwined moments of frivolous humor and sheer

Yeager leading formation of veteran pilots over Oshkosh, Wisconsin.

terror. An emotionally touched audience lingered following the presentation, reflecting on the historic nature of the event they had just witnessed.

In the morning, although the weather wasn't ideal, it was adequate for our assigned mission. As we taxied out under the heavy gray overcast, I felt strangely comfortable, squeezed into the tail of the B-25. I could see the familiar grin on General Yeager's face in the first Mustang, *Glamourous Glen III*, lined up behind us. Adjacent to Yeager, Pete Peterson wore an expression of concentration, as he prepared his Mustang, *Hurry Home Honey*, for takeoff. In the next row I could see Tommy Hayes' *Frenesi*, and Kit Carson's *Nooky Bookie IV*, but could not see their faces over the Mustang's long nose. Farther back, Bud Anderson pulled up the rear. Anderson's Mustang, *Old Crow*, was unavailable for the event, but he had been graciously provided with another so he could join the flight.

After takeoff, the five veteran fighter pilots joined almost effortlessly with the B-25 camera ship. General Yeager led the echelon flight with a relaxed ease, reflective of his experience. The formation of five Mustangs presented an awe inspiring picture: a combination of colorful personalities and machinery in a historic fifty-year reunion. I directed a diamond formation from the bomber's tail position, coaxing four of the fighters into symmetry in my wide angle viewfinder: "Yeager, move closer . . . Peterson, Hayes, tuck in on the leader . . . there . . . ."

Returning for landing, the adrenaline began to subside as it always does when the photo mission comes to an end. The indescribable grace and beauty of the subject, the nearly motionless calm of close formation, and the huge wavering circles described by the propeller tips have a hypnotic effect on the senses. The compulsive desire to capture the elusive moment demands the expenditure of obscene amounts of film. More often than not, I have had to stop shooting simply because I have run out of film. On landing approach, gazing out of the bomber's open escape hatch, I caught another fleeting glimpse of the image of the scarlet red Warhawk, surfacing momentarily from the subconscious, as if to refresh my memory.

Kalamazoo Aviation History Museum's P-47D Thunderbolt displays the markings of famed 56th Fighter Group ace, Francis Gabreski.

Grumman TBM-3E Avenger torpedo bomber.